PARENTING TODAY'S TEENS

A DEVOTIONAL FOR
DADS

MARK GREGSTON

FIRST EDITION

ISBN: 978-1-946466-50-1

Library of Congress Control Number: 2018954518

Published by

Certa
PUBLISHING

P.O. Box 2839, Apopka, FL 32704

In partnership with

heartlight
publishing

Printed in the United States of America

To Joe Mooberry, Bill O'Connell & David Muth,
three Dads that we lost this past year to whom I had the
utmost admiration. These guys loved the Lord and loved their
wife and kids in such a way that it was an example to all of
God's love being "fleshed out" to those near and dear to them.

Rest in Peace, dear friends!
Oh, the stories we'll share when we all gather again!

Acknowledgments

I can't help but acknowledge all the Dads that have been involved in my life through Young Life, the church I served in Tulsa, the wonderful people of Branson, Missouri, and all those thousands of Dads I've had the privilege to know through Heartlight. Your commitment to your family and dedication to living blamelessly while encouraging, inspiring, and imploring your children to walk in a manner that is worthy of God, is an example to us all.

A special thanks to all the staff at Heartlight and Heartlight Ministries who strive to look for new ways to offer help and hope to parents and teens in a broken world.

Thank you Roger Kemp, Wayne Shepherd, and Joe Carlson, with whom I have the privilege to work alongside with all our radio endeavors.

Thank you, Michael Blanton, a brother from a different mother, for your words of encouragement and actions of help that help keep ministry fun.

Thank you to all the board of directors of Heartlight who help make it all happen in so many different ways.

Mark Greston

Foreword

I was not prepared for the difficult, draining, and sometimes demeaning job of parenting teenagers. I should have been prepared. I have been a youth pastor and senior pastor for more than twenty-five years, and I have counseled countless families as they have walked this winding road, but I simply could not have imagined how hard it would be to walk it personally. I was not prepared! I stumbled, wallowed, wandered, and wondered how I could possibly get myself and my wife and my family to a better place. Frankly, I was lost...

...until I met Mark Gregston. While you and I have been doing whatever we have been doing with our lives, Mark Gregston and his wife, Jan, have been finding families in their toughest moments and leading them to help and healing. I will never forget the day we met—where I was and what I was feeling, needing hope and direction like never before. Mark answered the phone call of a stranger and rushed to our side as a friend. I received his name from one of the most well-known leaders of high school ministry in the world, who said, "Nobody understands Christian kids and their struggles or can help them and their parents like Mark Gregston."

Incredibly, that reference has proven abundantly true—it's even an understatement. A big part of Mark and Jan's gift is their faith. Mark and Jan are not stuffy Christians with easy answers, but they do love the Lord and believe that life works a lot better when the one who made us is shaping our thoughts and guiding our choices. Not just the kids, but their parents too.

When I have felt alone or confused or completely exhausted and unable to move in any direction, when I have felt trapped and misunderstood and deeply wounded, again and again as I have battled to a better place with my kids and our family, Mark has been there with practical counsel and biblical wisdom. I have often thought how fortunate I was to be able to talk to him personally and wondered how his practical insights and biblical wisdom could get to more people.

I am thankful that is now possible. Use this book when you wake in the night and need God's peace to get back to sleep. Read it in the morning when you want to get your day off to a good start. Keep it nearby at noon when the day takes a sudden turn and you want to stay on track. It contains biblical wisdom, mined from the wealth of God's Word, polished and ready to brighten your day and bring you to a better place as you wait on God to work in you and those you love. I am so excited to commend this helpful volume to you during these incredibly stretching days of trusting God.

Standing on the promises,

Dr. James MacDonald

"The Lord is good, a refuge in times of trouble.
He cares for those who trust in him." (Nahum 1:7)

Introduction

Most parents I meet love their teens dearly. They have spent a lot of time developing great relationships with their children and have worked hard to bring about good things in their kids' lives. They long to parent better, love deeper, and give sacrificially to those living in their home. Perhaps you're one of those parents who has given your all to your kids.

As kids enter the adolescent years, parenting tends to pose some new challenges, confusing situations, and unannounced opportunities. Maintaining your relationship with your child, whom you've always cherished, might have just become a little harder. The culture kids are growing up in might have ushered in some trials you thought would never be present and some situations that leave you scratching your head and wondering how to approach whatever it is that just entered your front door.

Parenting today's teens is not for cowards, not for the fainthearted, and not for those expecting to just breeze through the teen years on the coattails of the preadolescent years. It takes work, but if you keep the right mind-set, these could be the best days of your parenting, for this is the time for which you have been practicing. Now you can help your teen put into practice all that you have taught her as she takes a giant leap toward independence, develops her own faith, and encounters things she's never seen. Parenting today's teens is an adventure, an exciting and daring time when you might be pushed to the limit, use some skills you haven't used in years, and learn some new habits as you help your teen survive today's adolescent jungle.

Helping your teen navigate these turbulent waters won't necessarily require you to trade your style of parenting for a whole new approach. But you will need small reminders that God is still involved in your life, in your teen's life, and in your home during your teen's new adventure. Enter this devotional book.

When people ask me questions, they don't want me to tell them all the good things they are doing in their parenting. They ask me how they can improve on what they already know and are already doing. Anyone who knows me will testify that I tend to lean toward the simple, everyday, practical application of biblical principles and truths to develop the things we hope to see in our teens' lives.

So I'm not going to tell you in these daily devotions what you're doing right. I assume you know those things. Rather, I'll challenge your thinking about what you are doing so you can engage with your teen more effectively.

You have probably already encountered some of the topics in these pages. You might encounter others soon, and you should probably know about the rest even if you think you will never have to deal with them in your home. My thoughts in this book are similar to the thoughts I share every day on our daily radio program, *Parenting Today's Teens,* but I've added a few features to help you apply these daily reminders. Some pages contain a Scripture verse for the day to remind you of God's continual presence in your life and your teen's life. Others contain a "Thought for the Day" to encapsulate an important point. Many offer a question to think about throughout the day as you consider your parenting task and your teen's needs. And on many pages, you'll find short prayers asking God to bless our efforts to love our teens as He has loved us.

My prayer is that your days will be better as you seek more effective ways to interact with your teen when he needs you the most. May you be empowered to constantly adapt, refocus, contemplate, and engage with your teen in new ways.

I like to be heavenly minded and earthly focused. My advice is practical. I hope that you'll become more devoted to God and His principles and that you'll remain devoted to your teen as you experience and hopefully enjoy this adventure in parenting.

Mark Gregston

A Healing Direction

Teens do not have the tools they need to heal all their emotional wounds, especially their anger, pain, and loss. That's why sometimes they will try whatever pops into their heads or whatever their peers encourage them to do.

They'll take advantage of anything that is available to help dull their pain—including alcohol, drugs, cutting, or eating disorders. These behaviors may help them stuff their emotions into a box, but they take teens further away from healing and deeper into trouble.

How can you help your teen learn how to deal with pain in a healthy way? Start by recognizing the hurt. Validate its existence and stand with your teen rather than condemning her for having a problem. Then you can steer her response in a healing direction. This difficult time could be an opportunity of bonding just waiting to happen.

Scripture for the Day

"Pleasant words are a honeycomb, sweet to the soul and healing to the bones." (Proverbs 16:24)

Prayer for the Day

Lord, help me see with the eyes of my heart into my teen's life and to be the parent she needs me to be in a difficult time.

My Stupid Stuff

I admit, I've done some pretty stupid stuff.

I've been fired from a job and handled it wrong.

I've offended people when I didn't intend to (and when I did)

I've said things I shouldn't have said and yelled when I should have remained soft.

I've been extremely selfish and acted as if the world should revolve around me.

I've ignored what others have done for me.

I've been clueless about what they've sacrificed for me.

I've been disobedient, disrespectful, and sometimes dishonest.

I've lost friends because of my stupidity.

I've sought vengeance, prayed for revenge, and acted in anger.

I've done some pretty stupid stuff, just like your teen.

Perhaps just like you.

Scripture for the Day

"For what I do is not the good I want to do; no, the evil I do not want to do—this I keep on doing." (Romans 7:19)

Prayer for the Day

Heavenly Father, remind me of the actions of my youth so that I might be able to better understand my teen when he displays his age through his actions.

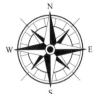 # Iwo Jima

John Wayne played Sergeant Striker in the 1949 movie *Sands of Iwo Jima*. One of his best lines has stuck with me for many years. He said, "Life is tough, but it's tougher when you're stupid."

Life is hard for teens living in today's confusing culture. Their world can eat them alive when they're struggling. And their lives get even harder if they do something stupid. Many times, parents interpret teens' stupid choices as rebellion when they really aren't acts of rebellion at all. They're merely stupid acts, cloaked in rebellious clothing. If you overreact to your teen's stupid decision, he just might decide to kick it into full-blown rebellion. So don't overreact when your teen does something stupid. Respond appropriately.

Scripture for the Day

"My dear brothers, take note of this: Everyone should be quick to listen, slow to speak and slow to become angry, for man's anger does not bring about the righteous life that God desires." (James 1:19-20)

Prayer for the Day

Lord, remind me of my youthful ways so that I might temper my response to my teen's inappropriate actions. May I help him get to a good spot and not rebel against my correction.

Just Different

Some teens are wired differently from the rest of the world. These kids need their moms and dads to recognize and accept those differences. Otherwise, parents can spend a whole lot of time in frustration, and their lack of acceptance will take away any possibility of having good relationships with their teens.

Realizing that your child is different from the person you expected her to be can be difficult. Accepting her uniqueness may mean letting go of some of your ideals, your hopes, and your desires. This leaves you with a choice. You can hold on to your predetermined expectations for your unique child (in which case, you'll constantly be disappointed), or you can adjust your expectations and empower her to flourish (which will help you to be content with the child God gave you)

Scripture for the Day

"I praise you because I am fearfully and wonderfully made; your works are wonderful, I know that full well." (Psalm 139:14)

Prayer for the Day

Lord, help me accept my child as she is. Help me see her as You do. Help me learn how to adjust my expectations for her and love her in ways that I never have before…in ways that often seem out of reach for me.

Princess Brawl

Girls younger than the age of twelve sometimes live in a fantasy world where princesses exist, and they may be convinced that they *are* princesses. And if one of these girls happens to be your daughter, you may agree with her.

But a kingdom usually has only one princess. Rarely do two exist in the same place, much less a few hundred—as can happen when girls start the seventh or eighth grade. When your daughter comes home from school and is angry and feeling lost, she may not be rebelling at all. She may just be a war-torn soldier taking out her frustrations on her king or queen (that would be you). Don't think she doesn't love you. You just might be the only ones left who believe she's a princess, and she might need encouragement that she still reigns in your home.

Thought for the Day

Your princess desperately needs you to help her rest and be restored. She probably won't handle her new frustrations very well.

Scripture for the Day

"But you are a chosen people, a royal priesthood, a holy nation, a people belonging to God, that you may declare the praises of him who called you out of darkness into his wonderful light." (1 Peter 2:9)

An Environment for Good Relationships

If you want a healthy relationship with your teen, you need to create an environment where it can develop. Relationships thrive in an atmosphere of unconditional love—a love that won't quit even when your teen doesn't respond the way you think he should. A love that continues even when he makes a mistake.

The secret longing of every teen's heart is for a relationship that helps him discover who he is and who he will become. Your child realizes this sense of significance through relationships that last—first with you, here on earth, and eventually with God for all of eternity.

Thought for the Day

Find a way to send this message to your teen today: "There is nothing you can do to make me love you more, and there is nothing you can do to make me love you less." He's waiting for you to say this. If you don't, he will more than likely find someone else who will.

Scripture for the Day

"Love never fails." (1 Corinthians 13:8)

Stay
Engaged

The teen years are not easy—for kids or for their parents. Teens, by their very nature, are selfish and prone to making mistakes. They mess up, they blow it, they get into trouble, and they cause trouble. They are just as imperfect as we were when we were their age. But today's culture has raised the stakes.

Have you made the commitment to stay engaged in your relationship with your teen even when the going gets tough? Even if your daughter comes home pregnant or wrecks the car, even if she flunks a class or gets caught shoplifting? Even if she uses drugs, drinks alcohol, lies to you, or cheats on a test? Will you stick with her even then? The easy way out is to disengage. Don't do it.

Your teen should suffer consequences as a result of her choices. She will lose privileges, but she needs room to make mistakes without losing her relationship with you. She needs your commitment, not your condemnation.

Scripture for the Day

"Surely I am with you always, to the very end of the age."
(Matthew 28:20)

A Sense of Significance

Parents tend to play different roles when helping their children find significance. Significance is knowing that who you are, what you do, and the things you say are important. Moms instill this sense of value, and dads validate it.

A child who doesn't experience a sense of significance in his relationships with his parents will search for it elsewhere—often in inappropriate ways. Your child may even do unbelievably stupid or dangerous things in his search for significance if he can't find it at home. He may violate everything about his character until he finds the acceptance he longs for. The poor choices he makes are likely to reaffirm or reinforce his childish thinking and childish behavior, and this creates another problem—peer dependence.

Let your teen know he is significant to you regardless of whether he's perfect or a perfect mess. Knowing that he's loved when he doesn't have it together will have an amazing effect even if he's strayed from what he really believes. It might just draw him back.

Scripture for the Day

"God so loved the world that he gave his one and only Son, that whoever believes in him shall not perish but have eternal life." (John 3:16)

The Definition of Security

Security is a convinced awareness of being totally and unconditionally loved without needing to change in order to win that love. Your teen wants to be secure, and the best place for her to find security is at home. She needs to experience a love that is freely given, cannot be earned, and therefore cannot be lost.

Your teen feels secure when she knows she doesn't need to perform in order to experience unconditional love. She needs to be assured that your relationship with her won't stop if she doesn't respond or if she messes up. And that your love survives the tough times. Now *that's* security! And only a secure teen is truly free.

Your teen's desire to be unconditionally loved and accepted is so intense, she may violate her own values in order to find it. So look at the log in your own eye before you judge the speck in hers. Are you telling and showing her that you love her unconditionally? If not, you might be pushing her to find security elsewhere.

Scripture for the Day

"Why do you look at the speck of sawdust in your brother's eye and pay no attention to the plank in your own eye?" (Matthew 7:3)

Structured for Success

I've worked with a lot of out-of-control teens, and I've seen firsthand how even a little bit of structure goes a long way toward restoring calmness in a home. I'm convinced that the 50 kids who live with me throughout the year actually thrive on structure.

If your teen ignores the house rules and bulldozes over the limits, now is the time to help him know in advance what to expect the next time he oversteps the boundaries. Sit down with him and line out the boundaries. Let him know the rules and the consequences for breaking the rules. Then he can decide whether to work within the household rules and whether his inappropriate choices are worth the consequences.

The hard part for any parent is to reinforce the structure and stick to the plan. So don't back down on the consequences when your teen violates a boundary or a house rule. Let the consequences have their full effect. They just might draw your child back to a better place and help him accept full responsibility for his life. In other words, he might grow in maturity!

Scripture for the Day

"In his heart a man plan's his course, but the LORD determines his steps." (Proverbs 16:9)

Peer Dependence

When your teen becomes devoted to new friends that you haven't met, you may become concerned—and rightly so. Peer dependence and fierce loyalty to the wrong kind of friends may be your teen's way to look for acceptance. Or she may be trying on a new persona to see how it feels to look and act a little different.

If you feel your teen has been replaced by a stranger, or if you notice some pretty drastic changes in her attitudes and appearance that worry you, she may have an issue with low self-esteem. Extreme peer dependence is one sign that your teen may need the help of a qualified counselor. That counselor might be you, it might be a youth pastor, or it might be a friend or relative. It might be a licensed professional. A qualified counselor is anyone who will spend time with your teen, accept her, and lovingly listen, comment, and steer her thinking back in the right direction.

Scripture for the Day

"Do not be wise in your own eyes; fear the LORD and shun evil." (Proverbs 3:7)

Prayer for the Day

Heavenly Father, please help me build a great relationship with my teen so she doesn't have to depend on her peers to affirm who she is. And please bring other great friends into her life so she can be surrounded by an accepting, nurturing community.

Rejection

Does your son refuse to spend any time with your family? Does he go out of his way to avoid family dinners? Does he say he hates your family even though he used to love everyone? Does he spend more time alone in his room than with the rest of you?

Is he connecting with others instead of you? Is the spark or gleam that used to shine so bright in his life now gone? Do you get an aching feeling in your gut that something just isn't right?

When a teen suddenly refuses to spend time with the family, especially when he also demonstrates a disrespect or hateful attitude, he may be spinning out of control.

A little intolerance for parents or family is normal in every teen's life, but when your teen constantly rejects your family, it's time to investigate, take a deeper look into his life, and seek wise counsel about how to handle it.

Scripture for the Day

"God sets the lonely in families, he leads forth the prisoners with singing; but the rebellious live in a sun-scorched land." (Psalm 68:6)

24

Overload of Family Stress

Are you a frazzled parent with a once normal and happy teen who is now decidedly out of control? Does she refuse to obey your house rules or ignore what you ask her to do? Do your simple requests just lead to more fighting or an overload of family stress? If asking your teen to follow some basic rules brings on nothing but conflict, or if every other family member suffers at the hands of a teen who refuses to cooperate, it's time to evaluate the situation and deal with it directly.

Adolescence is a time of challenging the way things have been, of moving toward independence, of questioning the family's values, of seeing if the things you've taught really work. That's normal adolescent life. And with your loving and consistent presence, your teen will get through it. But if she doesn't let up and the situation gets worse at home, start looking for a remedy sooner rather than later. An overload of family stress is one of the ten warning signs that a teen is spinning out of control. It may be time to get some help.

Scripture for the Day

"I am worn out from groaning; all night long I flood my bed with weeping and drench my couch with tears. My eyes grow weak with sorrow; they fail because of all my foes. Away from me, all you who do evil, for the LORD has heard my weeping. The LORD has heard my cry for mercy; the LORD accepts my prayer." (Psalm 6:6-9)

Grades and School

I never put much focus on either one of my kids' grades when they were in high school. I didn't want to be so domineering or performance based that I pushed them to give up. It's not that I didn't want them to make good grades. I just didn't want them to think my love for them was determined by their report cards.

I don't ask the kids who live with me now how they are doing in school unless it's to reassure them that they'll be okay even if they flunk a subject. I flunked a few, and I turned out just fine. If your child's grades aren't what you expect them to be, have a conversation about what needs to change and then move on. Let just one parent handle it. Make it a quick conversation.

This year, take the focus off his performance and send a different message: "You are valuable to me. I love you when you make great grades, and I love you when you don't."

Thought for the Day

I wonder...if parents spent more time rewarding their kids for good behavior and less time reprimanding them for bad behavior, would the children feel a greater sense of value?

Scripture for the Day

"Let us consider how we may spur one another on toward love and good deeds." (Hebrews 10:24)

Pouring Gas on Flames

Your teen may occasionally pull stupid stunts, and when he does, be careful about the way you respond. Some parents inadvertently throw gasoline on the fires teens start in their own lives rather than dousing those hotspots and extinguishing potential conflict. Before you respond to your teen, take a moment to remember some of the stunts you pulled while you were growing up. One day you'll laugh at some of your teen's stupid stunts, just as you laugh now at some of your own.

Scripture for the Day

"A gentle answer turns away wrath, but a harsh word stirs up anger." (Proverbs 15:1)

Thought for the Day

Most people think their first swing is their best swing. They might even think that what comes to their mind first is what they should say. Not so. Bridle your tongue, watch your approach, and move toward your teen with words that will effectively deal with the situation. Don't pour gas on the flames.

Prayer for the Day

Lord, help me to speak up when I should, back off at the right times, and engage in a way that will strengthen our relationship.

Reward Your Teen

You can help your teen learn to behave responsibly by rewarding her and praising her progress. Encouraging your child when she makes a good decision will empower her to do it again. Let consequences for poor decisions have their full effect, but never let good decisions go unnoticed. Offer praise lavishly. Let her hear your applause! Focus on her successes, not her failures. Give her more and more opportunities to make right choices. Keep looking for progress. Whenever your child shows maturity and responsibility, congratulate her and move her up to a new level of freedom as a reward. And keep in mind that instant feedback is always best.

Scripture for the Day

"The faithless will be fully repaid for their ways, and the good man rewarded for his." (Proverbs 14:14)

Thought for the Day

When my kids were at home, I spent too much time correcting them and not enough time connecting with them. When kids are corrected all the time, they move away and find people who will applaud their efforts.

Prayer for the Day

Lord, many times I spend my words correcting and forgetting to reward and praise the small things. Remind me to give encouragement, to use uplifting words, and to be less critical.

Moving Them On

Do you have a comfortable prodigal living in your home? The prodigal son Jesus spoke about came to his senses only when the consequences of his rotten way of living led him to eat with the swine instead of at his parents' table. But many teens today live a prodigal lifestyle while still enjoying the comforts of home. They get what they want and do as they please, all at Mom and Dad's expense. As a result, they never grow up.

Giving your teen what he wants may be fun, but it can quickly turn into enabling. Help your teen by requiring responsibility and enforcing consequences. Prepare him to successfully live on his own.

Scripture for the Day

"He longed to fill his stomach with the pods that the pigs were eating, but no one gave him anything. When he came to his senses, he said, 'How many of my father's hired men have food to spare, and here I am starving to death!'" (Luke 15:16-17)

Question for the Day

Are the things you give your child keeping him from growing up?

Prayer for the Day

Lord, help me to know when I am enabling my teen—and when to quit giving him what he wants.

Parents, Not Peers

Many parents in my generation have better relationships with their kids than did the previous generations. But we also get less respect. I respected my dad, but I didn't have much of a relationship with him. I feared him.

On the other hand, some parents are so concerned about having a great relationship with their kids that they abdicate their position of authority. When a parent acts more like his child's friend than a parent, he loses respect. Someone has to remain in charge and provide the discipline that leads a child to maturity. Your teen may not welcome your instruction or like the fact that you are training her for the future. But someday she will thank you for the maturity she receives from it.

Scripture for the Day

"Discipline your son, for in that there is hope; do not be a willing party to his death." (Proverbs 19:18)

Thought for the Day

How many friends does your teen have? Now...how many parents does she have?

Question for the Day

Are you better at being a friend or being a parent? Which do you think your teen needs the most?

Is That Normal?

Parents today sometimes have a hard time identifying normal and abnormal teen behavior. Irresponsibility, laziness, and mood swings can seem to be abnormal, but are they? Normal teenage behavior includes skipping chores, putting off homework, staying up late, losing things, and living on the verge of an emotional train wreck most of the time. These are aggravating to parents, but they are all pretty normal.

On the other hand, these things aren't normal: a sudden change in your child's personality, outbursts of rage or profanity, extreme disrespect for people or things, suddenly failing in school, not sleeping or sleeping too much, or self-imposed isolation.

If you see abnormal behavior suddenly appear in your teen, begin to ask questions. Spend some time talking with a youth minister, counselor, or teacher who understands the culture surrounding your teen. These discussions might help you understand your teen's situation, change your response to him, distinguish between normal and abnormal, and develop a plan to encourage the former and correct the latter.

Thought for the Day

If parents don't know what is normal, they will never know what is abnormal. Better to be safe than sorry. If something doesn't feel right, it probably isn't. Could the Holy Spirit be letting you know of a potential problem?

Communicating and Connecting

Teens do a lot of empty-headed electronic communicating. I've watched teens sitting in the same room send text messages to one another instead of having normal conversations. Many kids send hundreds of text messages a day. It's their communication style of choice.

This generation of teens knows how to communicate, and they have every device imaginable to stay in touch. But they don't always know how to make a more personal connection. And it's not something they'll learn unless you make a point to teach them. So open your home to alternatives: an evening of outdoor fun, playing board games, creating something, or just talking. Institute a LYPD (Leave Your Phones at the Door) policy on certain nights at your home. Demonstrate the difference between electronically communicating and really connecting.

Scripture for the Day

"The LORD is close to the brokenhearted and saves those who are crushed in spirit." (Psalm 34:18)

Prayer for the Day

Lord, help me make a truly relational connection with my teen. Make me a safe refuge for her, a place of rest, and a fountain of wisdom.

Love Well During Tough Times

Use your words and actions to love your child during the tough times. Tell him often, "There is nothing you can do to make me love you more, and nothing you can do to make me love you less." Say it even when he is at his worst and you feel as low as you've ever been.

Loving your teen unconditionally doesn't mean you ignore your own beliefs or rescue him from the consequences of his wrong behavior. You should never endorse or enable another's sin, but you are called to love the sinner, seek the lost, and help the blind— especially when that sinner, lost one, or blind one sleeps just down the hall from you. Unconditional love isn't affected by your teen's behavior. You love him regardless of what he decides to do or not to do. Just as God lovingly and wholeheartedly pursues us, gives us grace, and refuses to let us get away from Him, we can show compassion and love well when a child is choosing wrong things.

Scripture for the Day

"Let us not become weary in doing good, for at the proper time we will reap a harvest if we do not give up." (Galatians 6:9)

Prayer for the Day

Lord, I pray that I would be able to love, to share Your goodness, and to give of myself—even when I don't feel like it. Would you mold me and help me treat others the way You treat me?

Adoption Wisdom

Adoptive parents are often unprepared for the barrage of identity problems that may surface when an adopted child becomes a teen. My wife, Jan, and I have counseled hundreds of bewildered and broken adoptive parents. Many of them ask, "Why now?" Here are two reasons. First, as kids move from the concrete thinking of their preteen years into the abstract thinking of the teen years, new questions arise. Second, teens develop an extreme need to belong.

Adoptive parents learn the hard way that loving and nurturing a child does not always prevent her from asking, "Why did my mom give me away?" God, in His providence, may have given you the child He did because He knew how and when she would struggle with her identity. And He will equip you to help her when the questions come. This is an opportunity for you to affirm her belief that she really does belong to you.

Scripture for the Day

"Blessed is the man who perseveres under trial, because when he has stood the test, he will receive the crown of life that God has promised to those who love him." (James 1:12)

Question for the Day

Will you allow your teen to watch you handle your own struggles so she can learn how to handle her own?

Unconditional Love

When a teen is old enough to make his own decisions, you no longer have the power to control very much in his life. But you can manage your relationship with him as God directs, even if he exchanges a godly lifestyle for an unbiblical one. A good relationship with your older teen doesn't mean that you never have conflict or that you agree with all his decisions.

When you love your child even though he makes choices you don't agree with, when you set appropriate boundaries, and when you hang in there until he moves to the other side of the struggle, you give him a taste of the character of God he may not find anywhere else.

Scripture for the Day

"Above all, love each other deeply, because love covers over a multitude of sins." (1 Peter 4:8)

Question for the Day

Is your teen confident of your love for him? Is he assured of it by your actions, your words, and the way you handle your relationship with him?

Thought for the Day

When my son decided to get divorced instead of listening to my counsel, I was crushed. But I eventually realized that I had spent his entire life loving him only if he pleased me. God used my son's divorce to teach me an invaluable lesson.

Long-Haul Parenting

I often have to remind parents that problems like depression, anxiety, or addiction cannot be fixed with a formula. Overcoming these challenges may take more time, cost more money, and be more stressful than you ever dreamed possible, and you might not see progress in your child's troubled life for a very long time. In fact, you might never see her cured this side of heaven.

Instead of a quick fix, prepare for the long haul by continuing to ask God to do His work in your child's life, seeking the right kind of professional help, and surrounding your family with believers who know how to encourage and give comfort when you need it. Don't quit! Don't leave. And don't abandon this person who was and is a gift from God. She is still that gift.

Scripture for the Day

"Love...always protects, always trusts, always hopes, always perseveres." (1 Corinthians 13:7)

Thought for the Day

Perhaps God wants to use your child's struggle to change your heart and move you into a deeper relationship with Him. Embrace the struggle rather than fight against it.

Prayer for the Day

Jesus, help me keep the bigger picture in focus, understanding that my child's life will last far beyond the years that she is with me now. Help me keep her life in perspective.

Loaded with Laughter

Teens are emotionally overactive most of the time. It doesn't take much for them to flip out, feel upset, or become angry. If you don't want your home to be a minefield of tension, I suggest you find ways to laugh a little more. Start a new habit this week—everyone comes to the dinner table prepared to tell a joke. Even if you feel awkward or dumb, jokes can make everyone laugh! Vote on the best laugh and hand out a prize for the best joke.

A break in the tension is a welcomed emotional lift for your teen, and the whole family's load is lighter when they laugh. Laughter really can be the best medicine. Having fun, learning to laugh, lightening up a bit, and enjoying time with your teen builds relationship and sets an example. Teens often receive messages that most fun is inappropriate; laughter in the home corrects that misconception. And your example will help prepare your teen for the next stage of life—marriage, where learning to laugh once in a while is always a good idea.

Scripture for the Day

"He will yet fill your mouth with laughter and your lips with shouts of joy." (Job 8:21)

Question for the Day

Might fewer teens leave the faith if believers laughed more? Might this be part of the abundant life Jesus came to bring us? When is the last time that you had a good laugh?

37

Back on Target

Does your high school graduate seem to be floundering? After high school, some kids have no job, no plan to continue their education, and no hopeful outlook for the future. For some reason, they just don't know what they want to do or where they want to end up, let alone how they'll get there. They may fear the future and feel unprepared, so they may do nothing at all.

You can help your aimless teen by requiring him to remain active by finding a part-time job, registering at the local junior college, or even volunteering somewhere. You can help him create a plan that will help him learn to function in this new world. Gently building up his confidence and requiring him to stay on target will help him aim for more than a life on the couch playing video games. Keep your relationship intact, and keep pushing him on to maturity.

Scripture for the Day

"Therefore I do not run like a man running aimlessly; I do not fight like a man beating the air." (1 Corinthians 9:26)

Prayer for the Day

Heavenly Father, show me ways to motivate my child and give him a sense of purpose and a longing for life outside of our home. Help me help him.

Directionally Challenged

When you discipline your teen, you help her move in a direction she wants to go so she doesn't end up where she doesn't want to be. Discipline is about her, not about you. It's for her sake. When your teen knows the intent of discipline, she will be less likely to feel she is being disciplined just because you're angry with her.

So when you decide your family is not going to live in chaos anymore, make sure your teen understands that you are disciplining her in order to help her. If she begins to doubt that or decides she'd rather go a different direction, find someone outside the home to intervene and help her understand.

Scripture for the Day

"Do nothing out of selfish ambition or vain conceit, but in humility consider others better than yourselves." (Philippians 2:3)

Thought for the Day

Parents share their wisdom by helping their teens see the bigger picture and make decisions that will benefit them in the long run.

Question for the Day

If your child continues on the same path she's on now, where will she be in five years?

Offering Friendship to a Family

When a teen's behavior is causing problems, everyone in the family is affected. These days, if you're not struggling with teen issues, you probably know of families who are. Families in crisis get worn down and beat up by the turmoil, and if a mom or dad can't handle it, the family structure can break down.

A sense of community can help families in trouble. You can do a hurting family a lot of good by simply inviting them to talk about their situation or inviting them over for dinner. Don't wait until you can say something wise or profound. Someone might need just a listening ear and someone to sit with. Struggling is tough... and it's tougher when one feels isolated. Offer someone a listening ear of friendship in a time of need.

Scripture for the Day

"Offer hospitality to one another without grumbling." (1 Peter 4:9)

Thought for the Day

If you were going through some struggles with your teens, what would you want? A lecture? A book that tells you how to do things better? Sometimes a listening ear, a hug of support, and affirming words are the greatest gifts any neighbor can give a friend.

Finding Balance

D o we "baby" our teens too much today? By the time my father was 17, he was on his way to the South Pacific to fight in a war. Adversity in life forced Dad to grow up early, be responsible, and quickly learn to make good decisions. My generation arrived at age 17 knowing we had to work for what we wanted, respect our parents, and get jobs.

Today, most seventeen-year-olds can't even get out of bed without Mommy getting them up, much less make the bed or do their own laundry. My generation wanted to develop deeper relationships with our teens, but we've been weak on helping them become responsible and mature. The challenge is to work toward the right balance. So find a way to transfer some responsibility to your teen. If he starts getting himself out of bed, doing his own laundry, and paying for something (like insurance, gas, or his cell phone), he will immediately appreciate what you're still doing for him, and in the future, he'll appreciate the responsibility you gave him.

Scripture for the Day

"The fool folds his hands and ruins himself." (Ecclesiastes 4:5)

Question for the Day

What are you doing for your teen today that he will eventually have to do for himself? Would now be a good time to teach him and give him more responsibility?

Doing Drugs?

Parents today face a difficult battle raising kids when other teens are experimenting with every kind of intoxicating substance out there. In addition to alcohol and commonly known illegal drugs, teens learn from the Internet and from one another how to abuse prescription drugs and make mind-bending mixers out of their parents' medicine and liquor—now the number one source of drugs for teens.

Experimenting with any drug can trigger unexplainable changes in your teen's thinking, behavior, grades, and circle of friends. Parents tell me all the time that their teen changed overnight. Drugs and alcohol are the biggest reasons. Whether your teen is just beginning or has been secretly using drugs for quite a while, you must act quickly. Don't wait around for disaster. Find out through drug testing, calm conversations, or tracking your teen's whereabouts on the Internet, in the car, and with other friends. It's better to be safe than sorry.

Scripture for the Day

"The way of a fool seems right to him, but a wise man listens to advice." (Proverbs 12:15)

Thought for the Day

If you find out your teen is engaged in destructive habits, thank God that you know the truth and can plan a strategy for change.

What Are They Thinking?

Do you know how your teenager thinks? Honestly, do you know what she's thinking about right now?

Years ago, a wise lady taught me how to work with horses. She didn't give me a step-by-step plan to break and train every single horse. Instead, she taught me how horses think. Now I can find solutions for many different kinds of challenges that arise when I'm training horses.

I genuinely think this approach to problem solving also works with teens. Begin by learning about the way your teen thinks. Become a student of your teenager. Then you will be able to apply various parenting ideas more effectively in her life.

Scripture for the Day

"Then he went down to Nazareth with them and was obedient to them. But his mother treasured all these things in her heart." (Luke 2:51)

Thought for the Day

As your child moves into her teen years, your parenting style should shift from lecturing to discussion. And that discussion should be filled with open-ended questions that encourage thinking and invite a response. Practice your very best listening skills.

Foolish Overindulgence

I often work with troubled teens who have hit bottom and seemingly have nothing to look forward to. I believe part of the reason they feel that way is because most of them already have it all. Unbridled spending by parents hasn't helped teens feel significant or secure, and when real-life problems come calling, parents and teens are left unprepared. You may think everything is going well in your family because you have provided well for them. But when a crisis comes along, you may realize you've given way too much, way too soon.

Overindulgence is harmful for any teen. Instead of providing or protecting too much, begin to prepare your teen for real life by allowing him to work for what he wants. Let him have something to look forward to.

Scripture for the Day

"Remember this: Whoever sows sparingly will also reap sparingly, and whoever sows generously will also reap generously." (2 Corinthians 9:6)

Thought for the Day

We've all spoiled our kids in this affluent society. It may have been fun for us, but we haven't necessarily prepared our teens to live in the real world. We must parent with a bigger picture, considering how our actions today will help our teens to someday be married, have kids, hold a job, and be fully responsible for their own lives.

 # Wired Differently

Be careful to not allow a child with a unique mental, emotional, or physical characteristic to use it as an excuse to be disrespectful, disobedient, or dishonest. Even special-needs teens can learn to be accountable for their lives. Parents are responsible for finding the right ways to help children who are wired differently to grow up! You have a choice to make. You can simply hope for the best while your child with a difference constantly drains your energy, or you can find the right way to help your child make better decisions and take more responsibility.

Scripture for the Day

"What shall we say, then? Shall we go on sinning so that grace may increase? By no means!" (Romans 6:1-2)

Thought for the Day

If your teen doesn't think the way you do, and if you feel as if you're losing the battle for your teen, you might need to adjust your expectations and ask God to show you something about your teen that you've never seen before.

Prayer for the Day

Lord, my child is different. She is hurting our family, straining my marriage, and draining my life. I need You to show me a better way. Put someone in my life who can help. And Father, wrap Your arms around me so that I may feel Your presence.

Adapting Your Style

Being a steadfast parent in a constantly changing world is like hitting a moving target. Just when your aim is right on target, things change—including your kids. Setting appropriate standards and enforcing discipline when things constantly change may seem impossible. One key is to develop a more fluid and accessible parenting style.

As your teen gets older, you no longer have the luxury of making demands and expecting compliance. Whether you like it or not, things change, and you must adapt your parenting style and adjust your boundaries while remaining steadfast in your love for your child. Learn about her world and continue helping her see the need to be mature, responsible, and willing to accept the consequences of her choices.

Scripture for the Day

"Show the wonder of your great love, you who save by your right hand those who take refuge in you from their foes." (Psalm 17:7)

Thought for the Day

Parenting is an ever-changing challenge to meet your teen's current needs. Just when you think you have it figured out, new situations arise. It's a long obedience in the same direction. Don't give up!

Allow Him to Make Mistakes

One of the best ways to teach your child about the realities of life is to allow him to learn the hard way—to make some mistakes and experience the consequences of his actions. How will your teen ever learn to recognize good decisions unless he makes a few bad ones?

Great wisdom comes through learning from one's mistakes. So don't always stop your teen when he's about to blow it. Give him the freedom to fumble and learn how to get back on track. With each new bump in the road, he will gain something valuable, grow stronger, and be better prepared for his next big decision.

Scripture for the Day

"It was good for me to be afflicted so that I might learn your decrees." (Psalm 119:71)

Thought for the Day

Make a list of some of the good things you've learned from mistakes you've made. Your teen will learn similar valuable lessons for himself—unless you never allow him to make some of the same mistakes you made.

Ask a Question

God has empowered parents to influence two things in a teen's life—her thinking and her behavior. Of course, the two are closely related. Teaching a teen to behave differently means teaching her to think differently. The process starts in early adolescence and never really stops. Engage your teen's thinking by simply asking her questions and waiting for her to come up with the answers.

"Honey, what do you think should be done about that?" "Who is the best person to talk to about this?" "How much time should you give to this project?"

If she doesn't have an answer, don't give her one—just wait for it. If a good answer doesn't come the first time around, don't correct her. Instead, allow her to test her idea and experience some consequences. Let her think about it and come to a different conclusion for the next time. Then move on to the next important question, and wait for her to answer.

Scripture for the Day

"For as he thinks in his heart, so is he." (Proverbs 23:7 NKJV)

Question for the Day

Do you parent your teen by giving her all the answers or by teaching her how to find the answers herself? Will she be ready to face difficult questions when you're not around?

Asking for Help

Discipline is hard work. To formulate, communicate, and implement discipline that will get your teen to where he needs to be and keep him from a place he doesn't want to be—that requires thoughtful planning.

You look for progress and hope that your discipline is helping. But when what you are doing is not working, and you've tried many different approaches, it's time to ask for help from a pastor, counselor, or friend with whom both you and your child connect.

Don't wait until everything is spinning out of control before you seek guidance.

Don't clamp down on the rules in an effort to control the situation.

Don't give up and let your teen become a demanding tyrant.

Don't hesitate to ask just because you think it means you're a failure.

Ask for help! Not asking can get you in trouble.

Scripture for the Day

"Blessed is the man who finds wisdom, the man who gains understanding." (Proverbs 3:13)

Question for the Day

In what ways has our Lord been a good parent to you? How can you follow His example?

Be
Prepared

People in pain do weird things. Once I accompanied a dad to help him pick up his teen in order to bring him to Heartlight, our residential program, for help. We thought the teen would cry, express his anger, and then come along. A great thought, but it didn't really work out that way. Instead, the teen punched me so hard I saw stars. I looked up from where I fell to see him running away.

Soon after that incident, he made his way to Heartlight and apologized for giving me a black eye and a bad headache. We got along fine after that, and I never forgot that people in pain can be unpredictable. I didn't expect what happened, so I didn't prepare for it. And because I wasn't prepared, I couldn't handle the situation in a productive way. If your teen spins out of control, be prepared for the unexpected. And take a step back if you need to.

Scripture for the Day

"I am in pain and distress; may your salvation, O God, protect me!" (Psalm 69:29)

Thought for the Day

Parents tell me they weren't prepared to handle the changes in their teens because they never thought those changes would happen. What potential changes in your teen's life are you not prepared for?

Being Content with Whatever

Teens often feel that they cannot live up to their parents' expectations. They may feel that way even when those expectations are totally reasonable. Which begs the real question— will you be authentically content with whatever she tells you she wants to do in life? After all your hard work to get her where you think she needs to be, will you be happy if she decides to pursue something different from what you think she should?

Begin talking about expectations—both yours and hers. Develop a heart for your teen's desires, even if they don't seem ideal to you. Keeping your relationship with your child vibrant means keeping an open mind and sharing her excitement about finding and pursuing her heart's desire. No one ever said it would always be practical.

Scripture for the Day

"If the LORD delights in a man's way, he makes his steps firm." (Psalm 37:23)

Question for the Day

Will you still be able to love your teen if she chooses a path that is far different from what you desire for her? This is one of the toughest questions parents face today.

The Discerning Years

Have you helped your teen go through the process of making a good decision? Discernment is the ability to evaluate the circumstances and make a right choice based on the facts at hand. Secretly, most teens want their parents' help in making wise decisions, but they aren't likely to ask for it. They don't ask because they don't want to appear to be clueless. Instead, they want to appear to have it all together. Also, they don't want to seem to be dependent—they want to be able to choose their own path. So gently let your teen know you're available if he needs help.

Start by asking good questions. Listen to his reasoning but don't judge. After he has made a decision, follow up by asking, "Was it the experience you thought it would be?" Empower your child to make wise decisions by letting him develop the ability to discern right from wrong and weigh options. He needs to start making some decisions sometime. Would now be a good time?

Scripture for the Day

"The LORD is my light and my salvation—whom shall I fear? The LORD is the stronghold of my life—of whom shall I be afraid?" (Psalm 27:1)

Thought for the Day

If you've spent years training your child, is it time to let him demonstrate his ability to make decisions in the real world? Trust the work you have done, and trust God for what He will do.

Belief System

Teens struggle with arbitrary rules. To help your teen understand the reasoning behind your rules, find a way to communicate your belief system. This can be as simple as a set of statements that describe what you would like your family life to be like. These statements will provide the context and reasons for your rules without putting too much emphasis on them. They will also help your teen focus on a positive goal instead of the rules.

When your beliefs and rules are clearly articulated, the consequences for breaking those rules make sense. Share your belief system, stick to your rules, and when the rules are broken, let the consequences do their work.

Scripture for the Day

"Direct my footsteps according to your word; let no sin rule over me." (Psalm 119:133)

Question for the Day

The foundations of your belief system may not change very much through the years, but I can assure you this. The rules you establish to implement your beliefs must be subject to review. They will have to accommodate changes in your teen's life and adapt to culture.

Biosphere
Teens

Twenty years ago, eight scientists were sealed into a huge glass structure in the Arizona desert to see if life could be sustained the same way in outer space. Unexpectedly, the indoor trees withered because the biosphere had no wind. As wind bends a tree's bark, the tree responds by filling the tiny breaks with protective sap that hardens and forms a sturdy outer core, making the tree trunk strong enough to stand upright.

With teens, the winds of adversity come from making mistakes and learning from them. Overprotective parents produce overprotected biosphere teens, who, in a few short years, will fall flat when they take on a life all their own. Allow your teen to make choices and to make mistakes. This will expose her to some "wind" so she can learn, adapt, grow stronger, and make better decisions in the future.

Scripture for the Day

"For you have been my refuge, a strong tower against the foe." (Psalm 61:3)

Question for the Day

Can you think of any ways in which you overprotect your teen? If so, what does that communicate to her? That you haven't trained her well? That you don't believe God will protect her? That she is incapable of handling her life? Perhaps now is the time to trust that God will bless the work you've done as you've poured your life into your teen.

A Both/And Kind of Life

Smiling photographs are good reminders of the beauty in every struggling teen's heart. Remember those smiles when your teen struggles with intense, unpleasant issues. A teen once thanked me for helping people have fun. Even in the midst of struggles, look for things to enjoy and reasons to laugh.

When you learn to smile even in tough times, you begin to live a both/and kind of life. We're all needy, and we have no reason to be ashamed of our struggles. Life isn't either/or—easy or difficult, fun or challenging—it's both/and. But when we're knee-deep in difficult situations, we sometimes lose sight of the fun times and the laughter, the pleasant days and small victories.

Don't let your struggles overwhelm you. They're part of everyone's life, and they won't last forever. Anticipate happier times by looking for things to smile about.

I think I prefer the both/and kind of life.

Scripture for the Day

"A cheerful heart is good medicine, but a crushed spirit dries up the bones." (Proverbs 17:22)

Question for the Day

When was the last time your teen saw you laugh out loud?

Boundaries

You are likely to be annoyed—for good reason!—when your teen digs through your things, walks into your bathroom unannounced, or makes a mess and doesn't clean it up. Or how about when he demands things from you, takes your stuff, or throws tantrums when he doesn't get his way?

Boundaries are the fences you place around behavior in order to keep disobedience, dishonesty, and disrespect in check. Boundaries teach your child to be responsible, to respond differently the next time, and to learn from the negative consequences of his actions. Your teen will sometimes struggle with honoring your boundaries, but requiring him to do so is essential if he is to become a responsible adult. When he respects your boundaries, he learns the right way to behave in all of his relationships, and he becomes more likely to adopt some boundaries of his own.

Scripture for the Day

"Whoever loves discipline loves knowledge; but he who hates correction is stupid." (Proverbs 12:1)

Prayer for the Day

Lord, help me set boundaries that show where I begin and where I end, what I am to do and what I am not to do, when to say yes and when to say no. And help me equip the people in my family to honor each other's boundaries.

Changing Her Future

Wise parents understand what they can change in their teens' lives and what they can't. For example, you can't change your teen's feelings, and you can't always change her circumstances. What's happened in the past can never be altered. But her life in the future can be different from her life today. God has empowered you to influence your teen's thinking and her behavior. And your best tools for changing your teen's life are the consequences of her own choices.

Allowing your teen to face the unpleasant consequences of her faulty thinking can quickly bring her to new and better conclusions. So allow her the privilege of experiencing the full weight of the consequences of her choices. Don't pay too much attention to how the consequences make her feel, because she probably won't like them. Sooner or later you'll see her begin to think more clearly, make better decisions, and move toward a better future.

Scripture for the Day

"Do not conform any longer to the pattern of this world, but be transformed by the renewing of your mind." (Romans 12:2)

Question for the Day

Do you need your teen to like you all the time? Can you give your teen the consistency she needs even if she doesn't give you the affirmation you want?

Control and Limits

As you give your teen more control over his own life and he learns to make wise decisions, keep some limits in place. "Yes, you can take the car, but you can have no more than one other teen in the car—and be home by eleven." Don't go into details about driving safety and curfews. Simply set the limits and let him know the consequences if he chooses to step outside those limits.

Learning to live with the right limits will help your child grow in maturity, act unselfishly, and be less demanding.

Scripture for the Day

"Stop listening to instruction, my son, and you will stray from the words of knowledge." (Proverbs 19:27)

Thought for the Day

If your teen doesn't demonstrate internal controls (good judgment), you must maintain external control. But work diligently to help him develop internal controls, and when he shows signs of progress, reward him by releasing more of your external control.

Question for the Day

What are some ways that you are controlling your teen's life? Are there any areas where you can give him more control so he can develop good judgment?

Cutting

When teens are bored and looking for excitement, pain sometimes doesn't seem to stop them. Piercing, branding, cutting (self-harm), tattoos, cosmetic surgery, and over-the-edge reality shows are common in their culture.

Some say cutters are daring. I say they're numb and dissatisfied. Maybe cutting is a way for them to remind themselves that they're still alive. Self-mutilation and cutting may be symptomatic of mental illness, but not always. Cutters come from all walks of life, from all backgrounds, and from every type of family you can imagine. What was once confined to mental hospitals is now an activity teens use to cope. Sadly, cutting is a common fad and part of today's teens' everyday conversations, so don't be afraid to discuss it with your teen.

Scripture for the Day

"He heals the brokenhearted and binds up their wounds." (Psalm 147:3)

Thought for the Day

Who would have ever though that today's teens would cut themselves to relieve stress or to punish themselves? Who ever thought this type of behavior would become faddish among teens? Whether a parent understands the issue doesn't really matter. What does matter is that parents are ever mindful of their teens' activities and that they'll intervene when necessary to prevent future damage and find the root of this faddish behavior.

Damage Control

Have you ever asked yourself, *Why in the world is my teen behaving this way?* I believe that all behavior is goal oriented. Your teen may simply be trying to engage with the crazed culture. On the other hand, she may have experienced a loss that you are unaware of.

Your teen may respond to loss by minimizing it, denying it, feeling guilty, or feeling ashamed. She may feel as if she doesn't fit in, or she may hate herself for something she's done that she knows she shouldn't have done. Her outward behavior might simply be damage control for an inward sense of loss. Find out what happened, and you'll understand why she behaves the way she does. And understanding is important. It will change your approach to your teen's behavior, and it will give you a roadmap to follow as you lead her to restoration.

Scripture for the Day

"A happy heart makes the face cheerful, but heartache crushes the spirit." (Proverbs 15:13)

Question for the Day

Just as your parents probably don't know everything you did and everything that happened to you in high school, you probably don't know those things about your teen.

Prayer for the Day

Lord, make me the kind of person my teen wants to talk to about her losses.

Sitting in Jail

I work with troubled kids, and their parents often ask me what to do when their teens are arrested. I believe teens should experience the consequences of their behavior, so I recommend parents don't bail their kids out right away. This is a tough decision, but sitting for a day or two when they are young is better than facing a lifetime of imprisonments when they are older. Their time in jail might speak to them about their behavior in ways you never could and bring them to a sense of reality about the things they are choosing. Rescuing a teen from the consequences of inappropriate behavior sometimes only keeps him from learning a much-needed lesson.

So before you make a quick decision to bail out your teen, consider the opportunity for learning. Decide now what you will do if you are ever in that situation, and let him know of your decision so he's not surprised at your answer when he calls you with bad news.

Scripture for the Day

"A hot-tempered man must pay the penalty; if you rescue him, you will have to do it again." (Proverbs 19:19)

Prayer for the Day

Lord, I pray my child will never be arrested. But if he is, I pray for strength to do what's best for him, and I ask for patience and comfort while he is learning his lesson.

The Dark Weekend

Once Jan and I had a weekend that was so bad, we call it our dark weekend. It was a weekend designed to help survivors of childhood sexual abuse. We laugh when we talk about it now, but at the time it seemed unbearable. In the end, the uncomfortable truths we shared worked in our favor as we faced things head-on and with love.

Likewise, when your teen delivers overwhelming bad news, respond in a way that tells her that you intend to keep your relationship alive. Affirm that knowing the truth is better than not knowing. Hope waits on the other side of any struggle when you and your teen risk facing it together in a loving relationship.

Scripture for the Day

"Because of the Lord's great love we are not consumed, for his compassions never fail. They are new every morning; great is your faithfulness." (Lamentations 3:22-23)

Thought for the Day

Rather than walking away from people or shutting down to manage your pain, consider walking toward people you love and opening up to allow God's grace to heal you.

Prayer for the Day

Lord, help me remain engaged with my teen and my spouse as we encounter some uncharted waters in our family. Keep us close to You and close to each other. Thank You for being faithful.

 # Definitions of Loss

People experience loss when they don't get what they want, need, or hope for. They may also be deprived of something, fail to take advantage of something, be defeated by something, or be unable to maintain or keep something. Might your teen feel as if any of these things has happened to him? Has he been exposed to death or divorce? Your child's response to loss will show itself in his behavior.

Understanding the effect of loss in your teen's life helps get to the bottom of why he acts the way he does. Look beyond his inappropriate behavior, and try to find the driving force behind it.

Scripture for the Day

"My flesh and my heart may fail, but God is the strength of my heart and my portion forever." (Psalm 73:26)

Thought for the Day

Your teen notices the way you handle your own losses, and he will more than likely follow suit.

Question for the Day

How have you responded to the losses in your life, and how has that affected the way you parent your teen?

Diffusing
Angry Conflict

M y favorite way to diffuse an angry conflict with a teen is to agree with something she is saying.

"You're right! I mess up all the time."

"Yes, I am too busy—but I want to change."

"I know—I've struggled with that for years."

Then you can add your point.

"But you still have to listen to what I'm asking."

"And the rules about homework still apply."

"But I'm working on my struggles, and I expect you to work on yours."

Show a sincere appreciation for your teen's thoughts, and let her say what she really feels. Don't allow verbal abuse—take a break until she has more control. Avoid exploding; it will do even more damage to your relationship. And be patient. Your conflict may be as confusing to her as it is to you.

Scripture for the Day

"Hatred stirs up dissension, but love covers over all wrongs." (Proverbs 10:12)

Question for the Day

Do you and your teen process situations differently? If so, can you find some ways to adapt to her way of processing so you can all get to a better place?

Don't Give In

A teen who is spinning out of control needs a parent made of steel, especially when you draw a line that others may not support, agree with, or like. Remain involved with your child, and fight to keep the relationship alive, even when no one else thinks you should.

You can't parent by committee, so why try? Your out-of-control teen will think his behavior can continue unless you call a halt. So don't be afraid to send your child a message: "This behavior must stop. If you wish to remain at home, things must change." And don't quit, even when your ex doesn't support you, your mother-in-law berates you, or your best friend gossips about you. Continue to do what you know is right.

Scripture for the Day

"Do not fear, for I am with you; do not be dismayed, for I am your God. I will strengthen you and help you; I will uphold you with my righteous right hand." (Isaiah 41:10)

Thought for the Day

When you feel all alone and no one supports you, seek God's direction about your decision for your teens.

Question for the Day

What can help you do what you know is right when everyone is telling you that you are wrong?

Dress and Appearance

Concerned parents often tell me they are bothered by the way their teenagers dress—especially when their daughters dress seductively. Modesty is a virtue we need to honor, but I also know I hated to see my son wear his pants too low and his boxers too high in the seventh grade. When I was in high school, my dad hated my bushy sideburns, long hair, purple bell-bottoms, and boots that came up over my knees. Your parents probably didn't like the way you looked either.

For the most part, kids dress according to fads as they play out their roles on the stage of adolescence. Require your teen to keep it modest, but don't go crazy trying to overcorrect the way she dresses. The styles will change soon enough.

Scripture for the Day

"Don't let anyone look down on you because you are young, but set an example for the believers in speech, in life, in love, in faith and in purity." (1Timothy 4:12)

Thought for the Day

Music, tattoos, piercings, movies, and appearance can cause conflicts with your teen. Saying "Because I said so!" doesn't help. Good communication and understanding are vital.

Question for the Day

What fads did you follow that are now long gone?

Enlightened

Your teen will probably make some bad choices sometime, and finding out about them will never be easy for you. The way you handle your disappointment can determine the outcome. Will your relationship with your teen survive? Will he continue to struggle? How long will he remain in darkness? What kind of relationship will you have with him in the future?

Your teen needs to know he can do nothing to make you love him more and nothing to make you love him less even when his life is out of control. Loving your teen during tough times lets him know he has a compassionate advocate even when he is struggling.

Scripture for the Day

"And over all these virtues put on love, which binds them all together in perfect unity." (Colossians 3:14)

Thought for the Day

God can handle your good news and your bad news. Can you practice the love you've been preaching? Love well when it's easy—love more when it's tough.

Question for the Day

Is "loving the sinner" difficult when he is your own child? Why or why not?

Forgiveness Melts the Heart

When was the last time you asked someone to forgive you? I once witnessed an entire family break down and sob when the father asked each member to forgive him. He offered his request with intensity and emotion. It was a humble, sincere apology, and it was a good step toward healing the resentment of his children. Every heart in the room melted. Like this father, will you take responsibility for tearing down the walls of miscommunication and begin steering your home in the right direction, fostering positive emotions and mutual respect?

Start by identifying your offenses, and seek forgiveness from your teen or others in your home you may have offended. Next, ask them to help you keep a respectful attitude. Your teen's heart may seem impenetrable, but seeking her forgiveness may be the key.

Scripture for the Day

"Confess your sins to each other and pray for each other so that you may be healed." (James 5:16)

Thought for the Day

Dealing with the log in your own eye is never easy, but it could help you and your teen.

Question for the Day

Is anything lurking in your past that needs to be addressed so you can change the future?

Pain–a Little Now or a Lot Later

Athletes pay close attention to pain so they can avoid causing serious damage. Similarly, pain can help your teen know where not to go, and it can encourage him to make wiser choices and better plans. Pain also has benefits for parents. After all, families that face their pain together stay together in the long run. Unfortunately, some parents won't discipline their teens because they're afraid of causing pain. But wouldn't you rather tell the truth now and cause temporary pain than live with a sense of regret later, when your child is no longer in your home and you can't offer guidance and discipline? The temporary pain caused by discipline will go away as quickly as an athlete's muscle soreness.

Scripture for the Day

"Wounds from a friend can be trusted, but an enemy multiplies kisses." (Proverbs 27:6)

Thought for the Day

Many parents don't talk about painful issues with their teens, so they miss opportunities for growth and maturity. Their teens have to learn these missed lessons in their next stages of life as employees, marriage partners, or parents.

Question for the Day

Are there issues your family needs to address so that all can move into a deeper relationship with one another?

Giving It Back to Her

When you give your teenager some control over her own life, you help her learn through the decisions she makes. Even if she displays immaturity and irresponsibility or makes a really bad decision, don't be too quick to snatch back control and clamp down even harder on the rules. Of course, good parents offer some control and protection, but keeping your teen from making any more mistakes may cause more harm than good. Instead, gradually allow your teenager to assume more and more responsibility. Set reasonable boundaries and encourage her to make thoughtful decisions. Discuss more, dictate less, and offer advice only when she asks for it. Let the consequences of her choices speak for themselves.

Scripture for the Day

"Listen, my son, and be wise, and keep your heart on the right path." (Proverbs 23:19)

Question for the Day

Is releasing control difficult for you? Why? Most teens can handle a little more responsibility than their parents think they can. Do you think this could be the case with you and your teen?

Prayer for the Day

Lord, help me take control of my life and give my teen control of her life so she might learn to choose well in the days ahead.

God Loves Jerks

Does your teen ever act like a jerk? Does he sometimes imitate a disagreeable, immature, idiotic, mean-spirited, foolish nincompoop? I've seen teens kick my dog, dent my car, and break things. Their arrogant and annoying behavior is hard to take.

But teens have to put up with some jerks as well. These jerks don't listen, presume the worst, expect too much, want understanding but rarely give it to their teens, and hide behind their authority instead of dealing with the real issues at hand. I have been one of those jerks. The good news is that God loves us unconditionally, even when we behave badly. Likewise, you are never more like Christ in parenting than when you love your teen unconditionally, especially when he imitates a jerk.

Scripture for the Day

"God demonstrates his own love for us in this: While we were still sinners, Christ died for us." (Romans 5:8)

Question for the Day

How have you acted like a jerk? Will you ask forgiveness so the relationship can move ahead?

Prayer for the Day

Lord, help me offer my teen the love and grace You offer me. And help me not to be a jerk.

God Gives
Pain a Purpose

Has God given you opportunities to develop your character? Have some of those opportunities been painful? Some of the things I love most about my wife's character developed as she faced and dealt with her childhood sexual abuse.

God never causes abuse. But He faithfully uses everything for His good, for our own good, and for the good of those we love. God is in control even when we are in pain, and His Word promises that He will care for us during the struggle and use every painful experience for His good purposes.

Scripture for the Day

"In all things God works for the good of those who love him, who have been called according to his purpose." (Romans 8:28)

Thought for the Day

I was angry for years at a man who mistreated me. But then I dreamed that I saw him in heaven. I angrily asked God what he was doing there, and God said, "I've been using this man to help you become the person that I desired for you to be." I haven't been angry at this man since.

Question for the Day

What might God be using right now to make you more like Him?

Grace and
a Good Mood

Giving your teen grace is easy when you're in a good mood and he is doing well. But when your teen does poorly, giving him grace becomes more difficult. I guess that's how you know it's grace. In fact, grace is most needed when it's least deserved.

When your teen steps way out of line, crosses boundaries, offends you, and makes you angry, he doesn't deserve a gift. But that may be exactly the right time to give it. And even if giving a gift doesn't put you in a good mood, you can know you did the right thing.

Scripture for the Day

"For if you forgive men when they sin against you, your heavenly Father will also forgive you." (Matthew 6:14)

Thought for the Day

How would your teen respond if you gave him something he didn't deserve? Don't excuse his behavior or eliminate the consequences, but think of a way you can demonstrate grace by giving him something he doesn't expect or deserve.

Question for the Day

Is your home full of grace? When was the last time you extended grace to someone who didn't deserve it?

Great Expectations

Balancing your expectations for your teen can be tricky. If you expect too much, he will think he can never measure up. He'll bristle against your expectations and struggle with feelings of disappointment, discouragement, despair, and even despondency. But if you expect too little, he will think, *Who cares? No one ever listens to what I have to say, so why bother?*

Expectations can be a blessing or a burden. Talk with your teen about what's expected, be realistic, and strive to maintain a healthy balance.

Scripture for the Day

"'For I know the plans I have for you,' declares the Lord, 'plans to prosper you and not to harm you, plans to give you hope and a future.'" (Jeremiah 29:11)

Question for the Day

Does your teen know what you expect of him? Do you know what your teen expects of you?

Prayer for the Day

Gracious heavenly Father, You have told me of Your expectations through Your Word and have let me know of Your desires for my life. Would You help me do the same for my teen so that he may walk in a manner worthy of You?

I Told You So

Teens rarely ask for advice. Your teen probably thinks she doesn't need your help, even though you see her making the same mistakes over and over. Her quest for independence keeps her from asking for guidance, even when you and everyone else can see that she needs it.

If you offer your advice and she doesn't take it, don't lecture. If the first lecture didn't work, a second try is not likely to drive it home. And if you are ever tempted to tell your teen, "I told you so," bite your tongue. It's a shaming statement that tells her she should suffer because she didn't listen to you.

Even if she never admits it, she really is hearing your advice and learning from her mistakes. Your wisdom is more caught than taught at this stage, and your teen is trying to figure things out on her own. She'll eventually get to the other side of her confusion. And maybe someday, when she's a parent herself, she'll admit that maybe once or twice, you were right.

Scripture for the Day

"Listen, my sons, to a father's instruction; pay attention and gain understanding." (Proverbs 4:1)

Question for the Day

Can you think of any good reason to say "I told you so"? How do you feel when people say that to you?

License to Sin

You can give your teen grace, a soft answer, or a helping hand at just the right moment without giving him license to sin. Allowing him to continue his inappropriate behavior is never helpful. It hurts both him and the people he mistreats.

Discipline has two voices. The first voice says, "Yes, I offer you grace because I love you and want to stay in relationship with you even when you mess up." The second voice says, "No, you can't behave that way any longer without hurting yourself and losing your most important relationships." Grace doesn't let him off the hook and give him license to continue his unacceptable behavior. You offer grace by understanding his struggle, continuing to move toward him relationally, and letting him experience the consequences of his choices.

Scripture for the Day

"For certain men whose condemnation was written about long ago have secretly slipped in among you. They are godless men, who change the grace of our God into a license for immorality and deny Jesus Christ our only Sovereign and Lord." (Jude 1:4)

Thought for the Day

You offer grace to your teen when you don't excuse yourself from the table because of his sin.

Question for the Day

How would your teen define grace? Find out.

More Stuff

Parents give their kids more stuff today than ever before. Teens get cars, computers, iPods, TVs, cell phones, and more—and parents don't expect much in return. Teens are naturally self-centered, and regardless of how much they are given, they're ready for more.

But teens rarely understand or appreciate the sacrifice others have made for them. More stuff won't necessarily make your teen any happier or help her feel more significant. One of the best gifts you can give your teen is a sense of the value of working for what she wants! But she will never learn that as long as you keep giving her more stuff.

Scripture for the Day

"Keep your life free from love of money and be content with what you have, because God has said, 'Never will I leave you; never will I forsake you.'" (Hebrews 13:5)

Thought for the Day

I'm not against giving teens things. But if your teen never works and earns her own money, how will she deal with finances when she is on her own? Whatever you give your teen keeps her from earning it and learning from the process.

Question for the Day

Does your teen need more stuff? Why or why not?

Move It

Parents of today's teens must learn to adopt new attitudes and behaviors.

Move your style of communication from lecturing to discussing and from entertaining to experiencing things together. Instead of making demands, ask your teen for his ideas; instead of always requiring justice, give more grace; instead of pointing out what's wrong, find out what's right. Spend less time telling and more time listening, and wait to be invited before giving your opinion. Allow your teen to experience the consequences of choosing poorly, the detriments of crossing healthy boundaries, and the rewards for getting it right.

Your job is to teach your teen how to take his relationships in positive directions. But that won't happen unless you shift your style of parenting to meet the demands of this generation.

Scripture for the Day

"Neither do men pour new wine into old wineskins. If they do, the skins will burst, the wine will run out and the wineskins will be ruined. No, they pour new wine into new wineskins, and both are preserved." (Matthew 9:17)

Question for the Day

How have you shifted your parenting style to accommodate your teen's new needs, new influences, and new way of communicating? What changes do you need to make?

Out-of-Control Teens

If your teen is beginning to spin out of control, you need help. Start with a good counselor for you and your spouse. Then help your teen connect with a support person outside your family. Make it clear to your teen you will no longer allow the negative behavior to continue in your home. Issues of respect, honesty, and obedience are key. Reward good behavior, and allow negative consequences to have their full affect. Childish fighting is not what your family is about, so don't engage in it. If everything you try is unsuccessful, try a new approach. Many times, the conflict within families has little to do with the message and more to do with the messenger's approach.

Scripture for the Day

"My help comes from the LORD, the Maker of heaven and earth." (Psalm 121:2)

Thought for the Day

Fewer and fewer demands are placed on teens today. This relaxation of expectations sometimes entices teens to relax their obedience, respect, and honesty. Find a Christlike way to encourage change.

Prayer for the Day

Lord, help me boldly approach my teen with grace, understanding, empathy, and the expectation of better things for our family—in other words, just like You approach me!

Emotional Overactivity

Have you noticed that teens are emotionally overactive most of the time? It doesn't take much to make them crazy. Their world is pretty intense, and they can only take so much before they shut down, clam up, or get frustrated and lash out.

Is your child like a fortified city, a citadel with barred gates? Does she ignore your efforts to help? Or worse, does she respond with bitterness and resentment? When the atmosphere at home is tense all the time, your teen may never feel as if she can unwind. Help her by looking for ways to lighten up, laugh more, and enjoy life.

Scripture for the Day

"We will sing for joy over your victory, and in the name of our God we will set up our banners." (Psalm 20:5)

Thought for the Day

Find ways for your family to have fun and laugh together. Is it time for a family vacation? Your teen may not deserve it, but isn't that what grace is all about?

Prayer for the Day

Lord, help my family to lighten up and laugh a little more. Give me ways to assure them that You are bigger than all the junk they experience daily and that You are still in control. Show us how to laugh out loud, smile more, and have some fun together!

Pain Will Come

I'm not a magician, but I can predict when pain will appear in parenting. When you confront foolish thinking, when two value systems clash, or when you have a difference of opinion, life can become painful. Anytime someone lashes out, pain appears. When you need to reestablish your authority, when you expose wrong motives and desires, or when you confront, limit, or restrict your teen, both you and your teen will probably feel some pain.

Do you avoid discipline because you know it will be painful? Don't let that keep you from doing your job. The pain will pass soon enough, and working through things even though they are painful is necessary. Someday, your efforts will be appreciated.

Scripture for the Day

"Listen, my son, to your father's instruction and do not forsake your mother's teaching." (Proverbs 1:8)

Thought for the Day

Pain is an essential part of life that helps a teen mature and become responsible. If you eliminate or deflect your teen's pain, you may keep him or her from growing.

Prayer for the Day

Lord, most of my best lessons have been wrapped in pain. Help me allow my teen to learn the same way.

Pain's Perspective

I met a man named Mike who was losing a battle with cancer but winning insights about life that couldn't come any other way. When we were introduced, I asked, "How are you doing?"

"Great!" he replied. "I wasn't supposed to make it to Easter, and now it's May twenty-second!"

I said, "Well, that's an interesting perspective."

"I actually have a lot to be thankful for," he said. "My wife and I know more about God's love and care than ever before."

We are rarely able to view life from heaven's perspective. When disaster strikes your family, trust that your heavenly Father knows about it. Imaging Him telling you, "You're going to be okay. We're going to get through this together."

Scripture for the Day

"He will call upon me, and I will answer him; I will be with him in trouble, I will deliver him and honor him." (Psalm 91:15)

Thought for the Day

Pain has an amazing way of getting our attention, helping us focus on our Lord, making us sensitive to others, and helping us grow in Him. Surely these benefits are worth the discomfort.

Participation in Sports

A parent recently asked, "Should I ever force my kid to play a sport?"

You can help your teen by exposing him to an activity to find out if it's something he likes, or by giving him an opportunity he wouldn't otherwise have. But demanding that he plays a sport or joins any other activity just because you did when you were that age, or because you think that makes you a better parent...well, that's just selfish thinking. Sports are great, but they aren't for all kids. Carefully consider your motives before requiring your teen to sign up. You may find something else that's just as beneficial and that he enjoys a lot more. Remember, it's about him, not about you, right?

Scripture for the Day

"Let the wise listen and add to their learning, and let the discerning get guidance." (Proverbs 1:5)

Thought for the Day

Kids are born with likes and dislikes, just as I love coffee and not beets. If you want to help me fulfill God's call for my life, give me coffee and keep beets off my plate. Get what I'm saying?

Question for the Day

Are you molding your teen into the person you want him to be or encouraging him to become the person God wants him to be?

"Peerents"

I often deal with parents who are so concerned about being their teens' friends, they no longer look like parents. They look like peerents.

Peerents avoid correcting or disciplining, they're driven by their need to be loved by their teens, and they do anything to avoid conflict. Peerents permit wrong behavior in order to remain on friendly terms, sacrificing their teens' moral and spiritual growth. Peerenting misses the goal of godly parenting, which is to direct children to independence, self-control, and godly thinking. So make sure you're not idolizing your teen. Be her parent, not her peer. Allow her to experience some temporary pain or discomfort in order to mature, even if she doesn't like you for a little while.

Scripture for the Day

"Do not withhold discipline from a child." (Proverbs 23:13)

Thought for the Day

Your teen can always find other friends. She can't find other parents.

Prayer for the Day

Lord, surround me with people who can meet my social needs so I can meet my teen's parental needs.

Perfect Parenting

Conflict usually comes to an end when both parties realize they're not perfect and never will be. When Jan and I stopped trying to perfect one another, our marriage became much better, and we don't have much conflict anymore as a result.

Do you think your teen will suffer if you're not the perfect parent? Do you think your life would be better if your family never had any strife? The truth is, you will never be a perfect parent, and your child will never become perfect as a result of your parenting. Trying to create the appearance of perfection doesn't solve problems—it causes them.

Let your parenting strategy focus on your relationship with your teen, not on making everything look perfect.

Scripture for the Day

"As for God, his way is perfect; the word of the LORD is flawless. He is a shield for all who take refuge in him." (Psalm 18:30)

Thought for the Day

Being honest about our imperfection and our need for Christ is much better than trying to appear perfect and pretending that we don't really need Him.

Performance-Based Parenting

A re you a performance-based parent? In performance-based relationships, people's value depends on their actions or accomplishments. These relationships are filled with expectations that people have to live up to. Love is expressed or withheld according to the way people behave, so the underlying message is, "I won't love you anymore if you mess up."

Your child will breathe a sigh of relief when you take your focus off his performance and reassure him that he can do nothing to make you love him more and nothing to make you love him less—even if he messes up. Of course, you don't want him to suffer miserable consequences. But let him know that regardless of what happens, you'll always love him and value your relationship.

Scripture for the Day

"The Lord appeared to us in the past, saying: 'I have loved you with an everlasting love; I have drawn you with loving-kindness.'" (Jeremiah 31:3)

Question for the Day

Are you committed to move toward your teen even when he doesn't do what you ask him to?

Prayer for the Day

Father, may those around me know of my love for them when they have it all together and perform well, and may they know of my love for them when they fail miserably.

Praying for the Rain to Stop

Christians believe that prayer changes things. When we pray, life changes. We experience something different. Then we pray some more.

When your teen is going through a downpour of difficulties, you certainly pray for things to change, right? Do you feel overwhelmed by floods of emotion? Have some of your dreams and hopes for your child been swept away? Has a river of adversity carried your family to a strange place? You can't control some of the storms you're experiencing, but that doesn't mean you're helpless or alone. Just as you will never leave or forsake your child, God never leaves or forsakes His children. So keep on praying. God is faithful to work in your life and in your teen's life, and the storm will eventually pass. Things will change.

Scripture for the Day

"Land that drinks in the rain often falling on it and that produces a crop useful to those for whom it is farmed receives the blessing of God." (Hebrews 6:7)

Thought for the Day

There would be no life without rain.

Prayer for the Day

Lord, thanks for the rain. Would You make it stop now? Help me to trust Your timing.

Don't Provoke Them

When parents provoke their teenagers to the point of exasperation, they invite an angry response. Teens may never get over their harsh or demeaning parents, even later in life. Unkind and insensitive words have a way of sticking with kids and shaping the way they think. Parents' barbs cut deep wounds into the hearts of their children.

Everyone has moments of not handling things well, and even the best parent loses it once in a while. But if you lose it more often than not, recognize that you have a problem and get some help. This doesn't mean your teen is right, but your communication style might be provoking your immature teen to respond poorly. Changing the course of your relationship could rescue your teen from discouragement and keep you from living in frustration. You can't force your teen to change, but you can change your own communication style.

Scripture for the Day

"Fathers, do not exasperate your children; instead, bring them up in the training and instruction of the Lord." (Ephesians 6:4)

Prayer for the Day

Lord, I don't even realize when I am communicating poorly. Regardless of what I say, my teen seems to interpret it negatively. Would You show me a better way? Help me to pause and think before I speak and to stop talking before I say something I shouldn't.

Relationships
Are Forever

Being in a relationship with your child means being involved—rubbing shoulders both now and ten years from now. It allows you to communicate a better way of living, a different view of life, and the gospel of Christ. It prepares your teen for marriage and parenting. Your teen needs a relationship with you more than anything else you could give her. She longs for a sense of significance, and the best place for her to find it is in her relationship with you.

Relationships are not just short-term. Two things last in this world: the Word of God and relationships. Both are eternal. Relationships are forever.

Scripture for the Day

"We loved you so much that we were delighted to share with you not only the gospel of God but our lives as well, because you had become so dear to us." (1 Thessalonians 2:8)

Thought for the Day

Perhaps God gave you this child because He knew that when she became a teen, she would need someone just like you to walk with her through some difficult times.

Question for the Day

If your teen is lost or is becoming lost, who will she need to turn to when she finally wants to know the truth? You.

Scripture's Soft Answer

First Peter 3:9 says, "Do not repay evil with evil or insult with insult, but with blessing, because to this you were called so that you may inherit a blessing." Parents can become exasperated by abrasive teens who aren't afraid to throw insults. But the principle works both ways—teens sometimes bear the brunt of their parents' harsh words. Avoid teasing or inappropriate joking, reckless comments, and sharp criticism. Listen more and don't lecture, give your teen wise counsel when he asks for it, and refrain from insensitive remarks. If you speak when you should have kept quiet, seek your child's forgiveness and use a gentle answer the next time things heat up.

Question for the Day

If you're like me, you've blown it quite a few times with your teen. I teased, joked, and made reckless and critical comments. I had to say "I'm sorry" many more times than I was able to say "You're welcome." My teens were quick to restore our relationship even when I was slow to catch on. Do you need to ask forgiveness today for any harsh words?

Prayer for the Day

Lord, I mean well, but the way I talk doesn't seem to communicate what's in my heart. Somewhere between intent and execution, the words don't come out right. Would You help me be careful with my words, speak from my heart, and express my love for my teen?

Shhhh!

Proverbs 10:8 says, "The wise in heart accept commands, but a chattering fool comes to ruin." Nothing is more destructive to your relationship with your teen than constant lecturing. It will make her feel as if you assume she can't think for herself. She will feel demeaned and disrespected if you condemn her for her mistakes. So take a verbal step back before your teen stops listening altogether. To put it more bluntly—zip it!

Try it for a day. Don't flip out, argue, or try to change her thinking. Just let it go. Once you stop lecturing, you can start listening. You may discover it's something you're just not good at and need to practice more.

Scripture for the Day

"God is in heaven and you are on earth, so let your words be few." (Ecclesiastes 5:2)

Thought for the Day

Proverbs 10:19 reminds us, "When words are many, sin is not absent, but he who holds his tongue is wise." Do you want to appear wise to your teen? Find ways to connect with her, always be ready to listen to her, and don't feel as if you need to tell her everything you know. Eventually, she just might ask for your opinion.

Standards-Driven Christianity

Teens pay close attention to the way Christians respond to those who are struggling. Churches seem to reward teens who appear to be doing what's expected of them. But kids who are honest enough to admit they're missing the mark may feel a deep sense of shame—not from God, but from other Christians. Standards-driven Christianity sets the bar so high, it's hard for anyone to reach.

But doesn't God reach out to those who struggle and fail? Isaiah 40:29-31 says, "He gives strength to the weary and increases the power of the weak. Even youths grow tired and weary, and young men stumble and fall; but those who hope in the Lord will renew their strength." When teens are feeling lost and confused, the church should be a safe place for them to run to and find love, acceptance, forgiveness, encouragement, and guidance.

Thought for the Day

We should affirm biblical principles and encourage appropriate standards for our teens. But setting the bar too high causes frustration and deception. Make sure you're encouraging your teen and not discouraging her. And if she fails, draw her close—don't push her away.

Prayer for the Day

Lord, help me set standards that encourage my teen so she is drawn toward You and into the life You want her to live. Help me never to shame her and drive her away.

Starbucks Christianity

Proverbs 27:9 says, "Perfume and incense bring joy to the heart, and the pleasantness of one's friend springs from his earnest counsel."

I love going into the coffee shop. The baristas smile at me, greet me by name, and remember what I like—a grande sugar-free skinny vanilla latte. I enjoy fun relationships like these...and your teen is no different. He wants to socialize, be accepted for who he is, and belong to groups outside his family. Your teen needs your support as he attempts to connect with others. So don't overprotect him when he experiments with moving into environments in which you are not totally comfortable. Instead, help him connect and find good friends with your guidance and support.

Thought for the Day

Teens move toward people who accept them, make them feel welcome, and give them a sense of value—regardless of whether those people are acting appropriately. Can you accept people who make bad choices? That's what Christ did for you!

Prayer for the Day

Lord, I pray that You would use me in my teen's life and in his friends' lives. Help me to be a breath of fresh air for them—a voice of acceptance, a place of comfort, and a source of wisdom.

Silent

Proverbs 17:28 says, "Even a fool is thought wise if he keeps silent, and discerning if he holds his tongue." Do you honestly believe you can teach your child what she needs to know by being quiet? The truth is not only that you can but also that most of the time, you should. Your teen usually doesn't say much that is earth-shattering or profound...she's just processing what's happening in her world. That shouldn't require much of a verbal response from you.

When you do need to address an issue, try a new approach. Take your teen to breakfast and simply ask her some thoughtful questions. Your teen may find some answers in a way that engages her thinking and beliefs. For example, ask...

"I never thought of it that way. What makes you think so?"

"What do you think will happen if...?"

"What do you think is the best thing to do about it?"

And instead of always pushing to be involved in the discussion or seeking to give your own opinion, try keeping quiet and waiting to be invited to participate. You have wonderful insights to share, but your teen has to be in the right mind-set to receive them. Wait for just the right time, and let her be the one to open the door.

Prayer for the Day

Lord, help me learn when to engage my ears and disengage my mouth. When You are silent with me, I eagerly anticipate Your answers. Let my silence work the same way with my teen.

Teen Survival Mode

Do you think you'll survive your child's teenage years? Let me assure you, you will. The best way to survive is to make sure your home communicates unconditional love across a bridge of friendship that never ends—even when your teen makes mistakes or doesn't respond.

Bridge building includes spending time together, one-on-one, doing something he enjoys. Also, look for chances just to sit and talk. Make sure to keep your sense of humor! Don't be sour, bitter, and stressed all of the time. Lighten up! Tell more jokes and laugh out loud every chance you get. Believe in your child's future, and don't dwell on problems—deal with them and move on. And finally, correct and discipline your teen, even when doing so makes you uncomfortable. He won't like it at the time, but in the long run, your commitment to stay involved and address inappropriate behavior will assure him of your love.

Scripture for the Day

"A friend loves at all times, and a brother is born for adversity." (Proverbs 17:17)

Thought for the Day

Now is your opportunity to apply everything you've taught, demonstrated, and practiced throughout the preteen years. Enjoy the ride!

Prayer for the Day

Faithful Father, help me know how to build up the bridge that links me and my teen.

Tell the Truth in Love

Psalm 111:7 states, "The works of his hands are faithful and just; all his precepts are trustworthy."

In earlier years I transported resistant teens to our therapeutic treatment program. I'd locate a kid and then lie like crazy to get her to come along. I'd say her parents were sick, or they had been in an accident, or some other half-truth. Eventually, of course, I'd tell her the truth. But my initial lie about where she was going started my relationship with her down a negative path that I would spend the next six months unwinding. I had meant well, but my words gave the impression I couldn't be trusted.

I finally decided to always tell kids the truth—right from the start. Lying was easier, but it was harder on our relationship. Always tell your teen the truth, even when doing so is difficult, and speak gently and humbly.

Scripture for the Day

"I have chosen the way of the truth; I have set my heart on your laws." (Psalm 119:30)

Prayer for the Day

Heavenly Father, You have never lied to me, even when the news was worse than what I wanted to hear. Help me be as upright and trustworthy with my kids as You are with me.

The Barnyard Animals

Proverbs 22:6 says, "Train a child in the way he should go, and when he is old he will not turn from it." I'm confident this was written to encourage parents, not to measure their effectiveness.

That verse might more accurately be translated, "Train a child in the way that's right for him..." Your child has unique qualities that you must be aware of in order to properly train him to know right from wrong. Kids are like animals in the barnyard.

A mule is stubborn and unwilling to budge; a chicken is skittish and afraid to face reality. A bull thinks he's all that and pushes others around; a rooster acts as if he's the head of the henhouse. A donkey acts like a real...well, never mind. A pig makes a mess and expects you to clean it up. These animals are all different from each other and require different care. You can't feed a donkey chicken feed or expect a duck to live in the mud. A pig can't crow, and a mule can't swim (very well)

Likewise, your teen is unique and requires individualized care. His set of losses, his likes and dislikes, and his strengths and weaknesses are all unique. To train your child in the way he should go, you must know him well enough to know his "way."

Question for the Day

How well do you know your teen? How well would he say you know him?

The Next New Thing

I remember when it was scandalous for girls to wear jeans to school. That's certainly changed. And every few years, we see the next new thing come along. Hair styles go long and then short—and every color of the rainbow. Kids start piercing and tattooing any patch of skin they can find. Just when everybody is doing it, the next new thing comes along.

When your teen gets excited about the next new thing, don't worry about it or fight it, and try to understand her desire to fit in by participating. I fought with my parents about my hair, sideburns, weird clothes, loud music, and posters on my bedroom walls. It all seemed important at the time, but none of it was really that important in the long run. I wonder if some of the things we fight over today really won't make that big of a difference in the long run.

The most important thing to know about the next new thing is that if it doesn't represent outright rebellion or immorality, it's probably not that big of a deal. And it too shall pass.

Thought for the Day

Most teens adopt fads and engage in questionable behaviors because they want to fit in, not necessarily because they are trying to rebel. If you overreact and respond negatively, you may actually cause a rebellious attitude. Your teen may appear to be defending the fad, but what's really at stake is her desire to fit in.

Carl's Story

believe in letting kids experience the consequences of their actions—as long as they're fair.

I knew a kid named Carl who did some stupid things during his junior year in high school. Like most kids, Carl could have learned from his mistakes, rebounded, and carried on a normal life. But Carl's dad couldn't let it go. Instead of letting the consequences of Carl's choices do their work, his dad constantly hammered at his stupidity. Rather than helping Carl through a difficult time, he unwittingly pushed the child he loved further away from him. I honestly believe that if Carl's dad had handled his son's actions a little differently, things would have turned out fine. As it was, Carl rebelled. He left home and never returned.

Be careful not to make a bad situation worse by weighing it down with unfair consequences. Be merciful, and remember your youth—the times you were caught and the times you weren't.

Thought for the Day

Your response to your teen's mistakes will help determine the way he thinks about himself and the decisions he makes in the future.

Question for the Day

Are you walking beside your teen through today's difficult culture, or are you trying to stand between him and his culture? Which is most effective? What adjustments do you need to make?

Tom Landry's Approach

Does your teen run the show at your house? She shouldn't determine the plan for discipline in your home—you should. Tom Landry, former coach of the Dallas Cowboys, once said that a coach makes people do what they don't want to do in order to get them where they want to go. Such is the world of discipline. You are helping your teen get to where she wants to be and keep away from a place where she really doesn't want to go. Of course, she may not understand the purpose behind your actions right now. That's okay.

Disciplining your child is not an easy task, but she needs you to do it. If you don't discipline her, who will? Without your discipline, she'll have to learn even more lessons the hard way. So don't grow weary in doing what is right for your teen. Do what you know you are supposed to do. She may not like you all the time in the process, but she'll love you for your commitment when she's older, and your relationship will be much stronger in the long run.

Thought for the Day

Some parents choose not to discipline because they want better relationships with their teens than they had during their teen years with their parents. But the sad result is a teen who can't fulfill what she wants to do, can't get where she wants to go, and finds herself in a place she didn't want to be. Your role as her parent is to prepare her—and discipline her—in the midst of your relationship with her. It's not one or the other. Your teen needs both.

Tough Discussion About Living at Home

Your teen's behavior may deteriorate so far that you need to have a tough discussion with him about remaining at home. He might need to hear you say something like this:

We love you, we want you to be at home, and we will provide for you. However, we will not sit back and watch you destroy yourself as long as we have a say in your life. At age 18 you may choose whatever you want, and we will decide if we will continue to support you. Until then, we will no longer allow this behavior in our home. If it doesn't change, you will not be able to live here. We pray that you won't leave and that you will make choices that will benefit you in the long run. You're always welcome in this home, but some of your behaviors are not.

Asking a teen to leave home is tough. Most teens eventually decide that staying home and working things out is better than being out on their own.

Scripture for the Day

"Those whom I love I rebuke and discipline. So be earnest, and repent." (Revelation 3:19)

Prayer for the Day

Father, I pray that I will never have to engage in this discussion with my teen. But if I do, help me do so with love, clarity, a tear in my eye, and a boldness that conveys my love for him.

When Life Dishes It Out

Life has a way of dishing out trouble. You may be disappointed because things haven't turned out the way you thought they would, and you may be grieving the loss of a dream that never came true. In times like these it helps to remember that God guarantees He will never leave us or forsake us. In fact, the pain of dealing with a teen who is spinning out of control touches the reflective side of your spirit and causes you to focus on God's purpose and promises. He can bring good out of this struggle. When life brings things you can't handle, let it drive you to a better relationship with the Lord.

Scripture for the Day

"The LORD is a refuge for the oppressed, a stronghold in times of trouble. Those who know your name will trust in you, for you, LORD, have never forsaken those who seek you." (Psalm 9:9-10)

Thought for the Day

Pain is a well-intentioned gift from God that can preserve a life, a relationship, and a family.

Prayer for the Day

Lord, keep me focused and let me know that everything that now seems so chaotic will one day work together for our good. Will You also help me with assurance that I am going to make it and that our family will get through this time? Thank You.

Ten Minutes from Normal

Parents today sometimes have a hard time distinguishing between normal and abnormal teen behavior. What seems normal in your family may not be, and what seems abnormal may be your teen's harmless attempt to identify with today's bizarre youth culture. Learning the difference between normal and abnormal teen behavior is vital.

Most teens are pretty normal. They don't want to do chores for you but rush to help others. They put off homework, go to bed too late, get up too late, lose things, and listen to their music too loud. That's all normal.

But these things are not normal: a sudden change in personality, outbursts of profanity, extreme disrespect, dark depression, or a withdrawal from family or familiar friends. If your teen exhibits such abnormal behavior, it's time to get some help. These are undoubtedly symptoms of a deeper concern. Don't panic, but don't ignore the warning signs. Let them lead you to a better place.

Prayer for the Day

Lord, in an abnormal world, please show me what is normal and what is not. I look at the world and think that everything is going crazy, but then I realize that nothing is new to You. I pray for wisdom, knowledge, discernment, and most of all, understanding so that I might move toward my teen and not back away. I pray that in our struggles, You will lead my child and me to better relationships—with each other and with You.

Allow Your Teen to Make Mistakes

Did you know that your teen needs to be able to make some mistakes and suffer some consequences? One of the best ways to teach your child about the realities of life is to allow her to learn the hard way—to make some choices and suffer the consequences or reap the rewards for those decisions. This teaches her responsibility and develops wisdom.

How will your teen ever learn to recognize good decision making unless she makes a few bad ones? Her mistakes may be her greatest teachers because they provide plenty of motivation for her to make better choices in the future. So don't always stop your teen when she's about to blow it. Allow her to fumble and learn how to get back on track. With each new bump in the road, she can gain something valuable, grow stronger, and be prepared for the next time.

Scriptures for the Day

"A wise son heeds his father's instruction, but a mocker does not listen to rebuke." (Proverbs 13:1)

"A fool spurns his father's discipline, but whoever heeds correction shows prudence." (Proverbs 15:5)

Prayer for the Day

Lord, help me teach my teen to become more and more responsible and mature. And save me from interrupting her learning process, painful though it may be.

I Love You, Period

Every teen I've ever met wants to know he will continue to be loved when everything is a mess. Whatever the situation, the first thing to do is to move toward your teen, especially if he is in a tough spot. Let him know you love him, period. You may get frustrated, disappointed, or mad when your teen breaks the rules, talks back, or is deceitful, but try to separate his actions from your love for him. Let him know your love is unconditional and will continue regardless of what he's done.

Parents are naturally disappointed when their teens act inappropriately. But parents underestimate the youth culture's influence on their teens, and teens overestimate their ability to maintain control in the midst of it. Wise parents don't excuse their teens from experiencing important consequences, but they temper their response so that their teens feel secure in their relationship and don't have to worry about being rejected.

Thought for the Day

We all desire to be loved, especially when things are falling apart. Every teen wants parents who will love him when he's a mess. Teens must know their parents love them, period.

Question for the Day

Does your teen know that you love him? What's keeping him from knowing that? Would today be a good day to talk with him about unconditional love?

Grace

When your teen's behavior is way out of line, you might think she doesn't deserve grace. But that may be the best time to give it. Grace, given at just the right moment, can change the direction of a struggle and may even end it. Grace can bring your teen healing and restoration.

God's grace is His undeserved favor and forgiveness when we've chosen the seemingly unforgivable. In human terms, grace is an act of kindness, love, and forgiveness in the face of bad behavior or poor choices. Grace doesn't include lightening your teen's consequences or reducing her work hours simply because you don't want her to be mad at you. Grace is giving her something in the middle of her messed-up life, something that lets her know you still love her dearly. Proper consequences and plenty of grace can build self-worth and eliminate shame and self-contempt.

Scripture for the Day

"By grace you have been saved, through faith—and this not from yourselves, it is the gift of God—not by works, so that no one can boast." (Ephesians 2:8-9)

Prayer for the Day

Heavenly Father, it feels so wrong to show my teen grace when she has done wrong. It's hard to give when she has taken so much. It's hard to move toward her when she runs the other way. Help me to love even when she seems so unloving, just as You love us when we least deserve it.

A Different World

Teens in today's culture require a different style of parenting than most parents are used to. The world our kids live in is far different from the one you and I grew up in. They face unimaginable pressure to turn away from the values we have worked so hard to instill in their lives and to turn toward the enticements around them. Like me, you're probably glad you don't have to grow up in today's teen culture!

Raising kids in church, homeschool, or a religious school is no guarantee they won't struggle. Many parents wake up one morning to discover their teens have changed into people they don't even know. These parents can feel defeated and want to give up. But take heart, my friend. The world has changed, but God hasn't. His love, desires, and intentions are the same as when you and I grew up. Look for new ways to present a timeless message to your teen in a changing world.

Scripture for the Day

"Jesus Christ is the same yesterday and today and forever." (Hebrews 13:8)

Thought for the Day

God, who is unchanging, has spoken "at many times and in various ways" (Hebrews 1:1) so people could receive His message. Can you approach your teen in new ways to ensure the message gets through?

When to Disengage

Your teen may feel like unleashing a verbal tirade on you, but that is never appropriate. When he does speak to you disrespectfully, don't engage in a shouting match. Rather, simply disengage. Leave the room, hang up the phone, or stop the car and allow your teen to take a walk. This doesn't mean you should ever give up on your teen or break your relationship with him. But sometimes a little space can stop a bad situation from causing more damage. It reminds your teen that he won't accomplish anything by yelling. And it sends a clear message that disrespect is never allowed in the relationship.

So don't put up with verbal tirades. Next time, just disengage, and you'll put out the fire. And when everybody has cooled down, engage at a new and higher level of communication. Let him rise to your level of maturity—don't stoop down to his.

Scripture for the Day

"An angry man stirs up dissension, and a hot-tempered one commits many sins." (Proverbs 29:22)

Thought for the Day

I can't tell you how many times I've heard parents say they wish they had known when to disengage and let things cool down. Too many heated discussions can burn bridges.

Thumbprint

The child you brought home many years ago with God's thumbprint on her life is the same child you see today. Even when your family has struggles, you can be confident that God hasn't changed, and neither have His dreams for you and your teen. She was created for a purpose, and that purpose will not be sidetracked by a few bumps in the road—even big bumps.

So keep your teen's struggles in perspective. God can and will use whatever is happening in your teenager's life now to accomplish His perfect purpose for her down the road. You may not be able to see Him working, but He is. You may not know where He is leading you and your teen, but He is. Even if you feel lost, He hasn't abandoned you. God's thumbprint is still on your child, affirming her value, beauty, and uniqueness.

Scripture for the Day

"My dear children, for whom I am again in the pains of childbirth until Christ is formed in you, how I wish I could be with you now and change my tone, because I am perplexed about you!" (Galatians 4:19-20)

Prayer for the Day

Lord, help me see my teen the way You do. Help me see with my heart what I don't see with my eyes. Give me the bigger picture of Your work, and help me move toward my child when I am tempted to move away.

Talk About Performance

What do you and your teen talk about? My guess is that the most common topics include church, school, work, behaviors, privileges, and chores. Now, take a moment to consider what else you talk about. Pretty short list, isn't it? Most of what we talk about is performance oriented. Based on your conversations, might your teen think you value and love him only if he performs well?

Separating performance and relationship is critical. You want your teen to perform well, but his performance should have nothing to do with your relationship or acceptance. Keep talking about behavior, chores, academics, church, work, and such. But make sure you're also talking about things he really cares about—friends, relationships, fun, dreams, desires, thoughts, hurts, and losses. This will help him understand that you love him regardless of his performance; you love him unconditionally, just as God loves us. Don't assume he knows. Make sure he understands and believes it.

Scripture for the Day

"The good man brings good things out of the good stored up in his heart, and the evil man brings evil things out of the evil stored up in his heart. For out of the overflow of his heart his mouth speaks." (Luke 6:45)

Question for the Day

What can you and your teen talk about today? Make a list of new and fun topics.

Stop Expecting Perfection

In the early years of our marriage, my wife and I struggled until we learned an important lesson: Even though neither of us is perfect, we are perfect for each other. At first, we were driven to change one another, but then we learned to be content with each other's imperfections. We uncovered our self-centered reasons for wanting each other to be perfect. Really, I wanted Jan to be perfect— for me! How selfish is that! Our marriage is much more fulfilling now because we don't demand perfection from each other.

Likewise, wanting your teen to be perfect can bring disappointment, conflict, and stress—key elements for the perfect storm. Don't let her off the hook when she breaks the rules, but try every day to help your teen understand that she can do nothing to make you love her more and nothing to make you love her less. Does she know she doesn't have to be perfect?

Scripture for the Day

"Be kind and compassionate to one another, forgiving each other, just as in Christ God forgave you." (Ephesians 4:32)

Prayer for the Day

Heavenly Father, You are the only perfect one. Would You teach me some lessons on contentment and show me how to love imperfect people just as You love me? Thank You!

Social Monitoring

Are you concerned about how your teenager presents himself online? You should be because information he posts on the Internet can last for years and be seen around the world.

Do kids exaggerate or puff up themselves online? Of course they do. And sometimes they can also post personal information or threatening or untrue comments about others. Such posts can bring consequences for your teen or family. What happens on the Internet usually stays on the Internet—for a long time. That's why it is important to monitor or filter not only what your teen accesses on the Internet but also his personal pages and posts. If he balks, consider unplugging the Internet until he can be more responsible online.

Scripture for the Day

"Everyone who does evil hates the light, and will not come into the light for fear that his deeds will be exposed." (John 3:20)

Thought for the Day

Teens write things online that they would not say face-to-face. Keep your teen accountable.

Prayer for the Day

Lord, help me see the ways the culture is influencing my child. Open doors for us to talk about those things and agree on appropriate safeguards.

Root Causes

Your teenager may not know why she acts the way she does. She may appear rebellious but actually be responding to a painful experience—even from years ago. Do you know everything that's happened to her? Do your parents know everything that happened to you?

If your teenager is exhibiting serious behavioral problems, something in the past may be triggering them. The inappropriate behavior must stop, but I encourage you to seek help to solve the real issue and not simply change the behavior. A trained counselor can help uncover the root causes of her actions and attitude, bring these issues to the surface, and deal with them in an appropriate way. When you know how your teen has been damaged, you will respond to her inappropriate behavior in a new way. Get to the root and watch the behaviors wither away.

Scripture for the Day

"Though you have made me see troubles, many and bitter, you will restore my life again; from the depths of the earth you will again bring me up." (Psalm 71:20)

Thought for the Day

Most abnormal behavior begins with a deeper issue. Look for the root cause.

Prayer for the Day

Lord, help me look deeper and find the hidden causes of my teen's behavior.

Prepared for the Long Haul

Parents' unrealistic expectations cause as many problems as teenagers cause themselves. And the parents' issues can be tougher to address than the teens'. Parents almost always mean well, but sometimes they want to make changes, resolve issues, and restore peace...now!

Parents often think they can fix their teens' problems by reading the right book or applying the right technique. But every child is unique, and no set of simple steps can keep kids on the right path or steer them back to it if they lose their way. So if your teen is struggling, don't expect to find a quick fix. Instead, build up the support you will need for the long haul—support from the Lord and from gifted people He puts in your life. When the apostle Paul describes love in 1 Corinthians 13:4, he begins by saying, "Love is patient."

Scripture for the Day

"And we urge you, brothers, warn those who are idle, encourage the timid, help the weak, be patient with everyone." (1 Thessalonians 5:14)

Question for the Day

Is raising teens harder than you thought it would be? Rest assured, you can do this.

Prayer for the Day

Lord, let the fruit of the Spirit grow in me: love, joy, peace... and patience.

Marital Distress

D id you know that the stress of dealing with a teenager can affect your other relationships, including your marriage? The way you respond to your teen can change the way you respond to others. When the water is boiling, the steam has to go somewhere.

Also, teens can be experts at playing one parent against the other. One thing can lead to another, and before you know it, a family can be ripped apart. I've seen it again and again. If you think your marriage is immune from your parenting pressures, you won't prepare for the challenges you'll face or recognize the signs of distress. Be realistic about the strain you're under, and keep your eyes open. Don't allow your teen to dictate your personal schedule. Break the tension with regular exercise, fellowship, and fun. Most of all, keep close to God, who will give you the strength to persevere.

Question for the Day

Your spouse is probably the easiest person for you to talk to. Make sure you're not taking out your frustrations on him or her. You need each other to get through tough times, including this one.

Prayer for the Day

Lord, help me love my spouse more, and protect our marriage from anything that could come between us.

Getting Ready

I sometimes wonder if the reason we see so much anger in young people today is that we're not properly preparing them for life in the real world. As their horizons broaden, they don't seem to be ready to hit the ground running, and that unpreparedness angers and frustrates them. Maybe they feel as if they've walked into a class and been surprised by a test they haven't been prepared for.

As your children reach the teen years, focus less on protecting them and more on preparing them to be on their own. Do fewer things for them, and allow them to learn to do things and make decisions for themselves. The goal is to move our kids from dependence to independence and to prepare them to live well in a sometimes difficult world. If we do our job well, our young people will feel confident, content, and ready when they leave home.

Scripture for the Day

"These are the nations the Lord left to test all those Israelites who had not experienced any of the wars in Canaan (he did this only to teach warfare to the descendants of the Israelites who had not had previous battle experience)." (Judges 3:1-2)

Thought for the Day

Children need to learn how to handle small doses of rejection, ridicule, pain, and conflict over a long period of time to develop skills to handle that which they will face in their adolescent years.

Got a Cat by the Tail?

Are you frustrated with how little your teenager listens to your advice? Well, don't be. A parent can suddenly appear to be wise when a teenager has just learned a lesson the hard way. Mark Twain once said, "A man who carries a cat by the tail learns something he can learn no other way." Parents can lecture, warn, and talk till they're blue in the face, but nothing teaches a teenager better than firsthand experience.

So if your teen closes his ears to your counsel, my advice is to offer your help and then step out of the way and allow him to learn the hard way. He'll probably get a lesson he'll never forget. And it will move your teen toward you in the future as he seeks your guidance and wisdom. Be patient with him, and he'll soon learn of your importance and remember what you've taught him.

Scripture for the Day

"Before I was afflicted I went astray, but now I obey your word." (Psalm 119:67)

Question for the Day

What things might your teen learn better from others than from you?

Prayer for the Day

Lord, help me step in when my teen needs my help and step out when he doesn't.

Be on the Same Page

If I were determined to correct every issue a teenager presents, I would spend all my time correcting her and very little time building a relationship with her. Neither you nor your child are going to be perfect this side of heaven, and you'll have plenty of time to correct things along the way, so pick your battles wisely. Remember Einstein's perspective on time: "The purpose of time is to prevent everything from happening at once."

Determine what you need to teach now and what can wait. Then you can decide how you will confront issues and what the consequences will be. Focusing on the lessons that are important for your teenager to learn at this particular stage of the game will help ensure that everyone is on the same page and that relationships remain intact.

Scripture for the Day

"Make my joy complete by being like-minded, having the same love, being one in spirit and purpose." (Philippians 2:2)

Question for the Day

Are you spending too much time correcting and not enough time building a relationship?

Prayer for the Day

Father, help my spouse and me to agree about when to deal with various issues in our teen's life.

The Comfortable Prodigal

The prodigal Jesus spoke about came to his senses when he found himself sleeping in a pigpen instead of his parents' comfortable home. The consequences of his choices woke him up. Today, many prodigals won't leave home, or they make their own rules while living in their parents' homes. These teens get what they want and do as they please. Unfortunately, the parents allow this behavior and even feed it in the name of love and tolerance, so the teens never come to their senses. As a result, selfishness escalates, and the relationship is destroyed. If you want to help your prodigal, stop feeding his foolish appetites and start enforcing appropriate consequences. These are hard things for a loving parent to do, but they just may save your teen's life. He will learn the error of his ways, the result of his selfishness, and the importance of respect.

Scripture for the Day

"The rod of correction imparts wisdom, but a child left to himself disgraces his mother." (Proverbs 29:15)

Thought for the Day

If you have a prodigal in your home, bring the uncontrolled selfishness to a stop. Why wait?

Prayer for the Day

Jesus, You understand my predicament. Help me be as wise and strong as the prodigal's father.

Rampages

believe that young people who go on shooting rampages do so for two reasons: They feel hopeless, and they feel abandoned. They want others to feel the pain they have been carrying for years and to pay for their misery. These shooting incidents are rare, but they should cause us all to ask how they could have been prevented.

Do you know a teenager who is caught up in despair? Befriending that teen and offering him regular encouragement may not only save a young life but also keep your community from witnessing the next horrific shooting incident.

Scripture for the Day

"He said to them, 'Go into all the world and preach the good news to all creation.'" (Mark 16:15)

Thought for the Day

Many parents are concerned about the young people their teens spend time with—and rightly so. But instead of eliminating some of these kids from your teen's circle of friends, try embracing these needy teens and surrounding them with your love and nurture. You can win their hearts by showing them a love they may have never experienced.

Question for the Day

Could God use you in the life of one teen, causing a ripple effect of blessing?

Love Well During Tough Times

Your words and actions will demonstrate your love for your teenager during the tough times. Just as God lovingly and wholeheartedly pursues us, gives us grace, and refuses to let us get away from Him, we can show compassion and build a relationship even when a child chooses wrong behaviors, attitudes, friends, and lifestyles.

Loving unconditionally doesn't mean you ignore your own beliefs and boundaries or that you excuse your teen from the consequences of her behavior. Rather, it means that your love for her isn't affected by her behavior. You love her regardless of what she decides to do or not to do. Even when she makes poor decisions or turns her back on God, you continue to build your relationship.

Scripture for the Day

"I am convinced that neither death nor life, neither angels nor demons, neither the present nor the future, nor any powers, neither height nor depth, nor anything else in all creation, will be able to separate us from the love of God that is in Christ Jesus our Lord." (Romans 8:38-39)

Prayer for the Day

Lord, help me love my teen more each day than I did the day before. Show me how to build our relationship even while letting her experience the consequences of her behavior. May she never be separated from my love, just as she and I are never separated from Yours.

On the Other Side

When a teenager becomes an adult and leaves the home to live on his own, you no longer are able to control much in his life. You can, however, manage your relationship with him. Strong parent-child relationships are built on unconditional love— love that extends across a bridge of friendship that doesn't end when one person chooses poorly.

Loving unconditionally doesn't mean you ignore your own beliefs. Rather, it means you continue to build the relationship even when he's reaping what he's sown. That's not easy. Loving him when he's violating your principles can be challenging. You might be tempted to take the easy way out and just disengage. But if you do, you eliminate the possibility of him returning to you and to what you hope for him, possibly keeping him in his destructive lifestyle. So keep praying, and eventually your teen will come to his senses. When he does, he will need to know you'll still be there for him on the other side of the struggle.

Scripture for the Day

"Those who oppose him he must gently instruct, in the hope that God will grant them repentance leading them to a knowledge of the truth, and that they will come to their senses and escape from the trap of the devil, who has taken them captive to do his will." (2 Timothy 2:25-26)

Prayer for the Day

Lord, help me love my teen as You love me.

Riding in a Stunt Plane

I once took a ride in a stunt plane that I'll never forget. We climbed straight up into the sky, stalled, fell backward, and started spinning back to earth. I was horrified, threw up twice in just a few seconds, and couldn't breathe. I thought I was going to die. But when I looked at the pilot—a fellow I had known for years—I realized he was in complete control. I tried to loosen up a bit and smile as I threw up again.

When your teen seems out of control, you may feel as if you're in a free fall. You could become so disoriented, you don't know which way is up. But God is in control regardless of how you feel. You'll find a measure of peace and joy when you focus on God in the pilot's seat. He knows and sees what's happening in your teen's life, and He promises that every twist, turn, loop, and roll has a purpose in His flight plan.

Scripture for the Day

"The plans of the LORD stand firm forever, the purposes of his heart through all generations." (Psalm 33:11)

Prayer for the Day

Lord, it's an amazing ride! Help me not to follow my feelings, but to lean on Your promise that You are in control.

Making the Connection

Teens do a lot of meaningless communicating today. One mother recently told me her teen texted more than 9000 times in the previous month. My fingers feel worn out just thinking about it!

Twittering one-line communiqués is a teen's way to cry out, "Look at me, I'm important!" Nothing is wrong with communicating electronically as long as that's not the *only* way your teen communicates. She needs to connect with others, not just send messages. She may know how to stay in touch on every device imaginable and still not know how to build a relationship. She needs to learn that from you.

So invite her friends over for an evening to play board games, create something, or just talk. Go for a walk, experience something together, have long discussions, or go fishing. Turn off all the electronics and have your guests check their cell phones at the door. You'll be helping them to learn the joy and value of personally connecting—without using electronics.

Question for the Day

Do you just communicate with your teen, or do you actually connect with her?

Prayer for the Day

Heavenly Father, help me build a strong connection with my teen so that our relationship might flourish.

 # Rest for His Soul

A re you adding to your teenager's stress, or can he come to you to find refreshment? Can you identify his emotional needs and help him meet those needs constructively? If you can, you will give him a break from his confusing culture and bring rest to his soul.

Your teen has many pressures and conflicting values to sort out. You would do well to emulate Christ, who offered His followers this invitation: "If anyone is thirsty, let him come to me and drink" (John 7:37). Your relationship with your teen can provide a safe, comfortable place for him to find unconditional love and refreshment for his soul.

Scripture for the Day

"Come to me, all you who are weary and burdened, and I will give you rest. Take my yoke upon you and learn from me, for I am gentle and humble in heart, and you will find rest for your souls. For my yoke is easy and my burden is light." (Matthew 11:28-30)

Thought for the Day

This is a balancing act: Help your teen find rest and comfort in your home, but require him to accept certain standards of behavior.

Prayer for the Day

Lord, help my teen find comfort, rest, and refreshment in You and in me.

Friendship in a Time of Need

When a teenager causes problems in the family, she isn't the only one in need. The parents may desperately need support as well. Most parents in the midst of such storms become emotionally battered and worn down. They are often too embarrassed to reveal their situation to others, though people can easily see that something is wrong. The stress can even lead to the breakup of the family. But you can help parents like these by inviting them to confidentially talk to you about their situation. Don't give advice— just listen. And make a point of getting together once a week. In this simple way you can help break the tension and offer friendship and a listening ear in their time of need.

Scripture for the Day

"We have this treasure in jars of clay to show that this all-surpassing power is from God and not from us...We always carry around in our body the death of Jesus, so that the life of Jesus may also be revealed in our body." (2 Corinthians 4:7,10)

Thought for the Day

Hurting people are all around us. Our first mission field is in our own backyard.

Question for the Day

What can you use to build a connection with a hurting neighbor?

Love + Grace + Truth = Maturity

There is no right formula for bringing your teenager to maturity, but three elements will help you do a pretty good job of it. First, *unconditional love* lets him know he can do nothing to make you love him more and nothing to make you love him less. Second, *grace* gives him room to fail and the encouragement to learn from his mistakes. And third, *truth* reveals what is right and wrong and brings consequences to bear when he goes over the line.

Love, grace, and truth are three powerful ingredients that you can always apply generously.

Scripture for the Day

"Grace, mercy and peace from God the Father and from Jesus Christ, the Father's Son, will be with us in truth and love." (2 John 1:3)

Question for the Day

Which one of these three elements do you need to emphasize in your relationship with your teen?

Prayer for the Day

Lord, I pray Your bountiful and wondrous grace will fall on me today, and may it overflow from me onto my teen. Your love, grace, and truth sustain me, and for that I am most thankful.

Dilemma of Denial

Teens may believe their parents don't even know how much they don't know. But parents of teens often *do* know, deep in their souls, when something is not quite right with their teen. Call it a sixth sense or intuition. Or perhaps the Holy Spirit is nudging them to a deeper involvement in their teens' lives.

When you ignore these intuitions and unexplained feelings, you could be living in denial. Denial is usually a way of protecting yourself from the truth. But if your teen happens to be involved in a secret lifestyle, your denial can be deadly. So start listening to your heart. Trust the Spirit's gentle nudging. Kids today have easy access to a lot of very destructive things, and some will try these things out, so if you feel that something is wrong, it may well be. Get to the root of the problem before it gets out of hand. The time is now.

Thought for the Day

Denial isn't just a river in Egypt. It's the way to avoid the pain of not knowing what to do or having to deal with unpleasant situations! But God knows what to do, and He can deal with unpleasant things. He'll help you know what to do and give you the strength to do it.

Scripture for the Day

"Do you have eyes but fail to see, and ears but fail to hear?" (Mark 8:18)

Weary from Worry

Matthew 6:27 says, "Who of you by worrying can add a single hour to his life?" It's hard not to worry when your child is behaving in unacceptable ways or when you are faced with issues you never had to face as a teen. But when you worry, you misuse your imagination and mistrust God. He may be allowing your teen to struggle so you can learn that He is in control and that you can trust Him. The struggle your teen encounters in life can push him toward the Savior.

Jeremiah 17 encourages us by saying, "Blessed is the man who trusts in the LORD." Are you weary from worry, or do you trust God for every part of your teen's existence?

Scripture for the Day

"Do not worry about tomorrow, for tomorrow will worry about itself. Each day has enough trouble of its own." (Matthew 6:34)

Question for the Day

What has you worried about your teen? Can you pray specifically about your concern?

Prayer for the Day

Lord, help me not to worry about my teen and instead to trust You in the midst of my doubt. May I shine a beacon of hope to my teen and demonstrate that trusting You is much better than worrying.

Just Kidding

Proverbs 26:18-19 says, "Like a madman shooting firebrands or deadly arrows is a man who deceives his neighbor and says, 'I was only joking!'"

I used to joke around constantly, but then one day my daughter asked, "Why do you joke all the time? Why can't you be serious?" My attempts to be funny were damaging my teens. Family teasing at one member's expense is often inappropriate and damaging to self-worth, especially during the teen years. I'm all for having fun with one another and even making fun of one another as long as it remains good-natured and agreeable to all involved. But don't allow family members to make someone in your family the brunt of family jokes or use words that damage her self-esteem. In the end, it's just not that funny, especially to the person on the receiving end.

Scripture for the Day

"The tongue is a small part of the body, but it makes great boasts. Consider what a great forest is set on fire by a small spark. The tongue also is a fire, a world of evil among the parts of the body. It corrupts the whole person, sets the whole course of his life on fire, and is itself set on fire by hell." (James 3:5-6)

Prayer for the Day

Lord, help me tame my tongue and keep it from becoming a restless evil, full of deadly poison. Fill my heart with love that flows out in my words.

Prodigal Pirates

The year 2008 brought us the timeless classic, *The Pirates Who Don't Do Anything: A Veggie Tales Movie.* Sounds like some eighteen-year-olds I've met. They'd rather just stay at home, lie around, play video games, and watch movies. These older teens are happy to remain in a high school mind-set, not doing much of anything after high school graduation, all at Mom and Dad's expense. In plenty of these cases, Mom and Dad have quit providing and started enabling.

Taking a vacation after high school is normal. Retiring after high school is not normal. Parents need to teach their teens that graduation is a beginning. I always encourage parents to come up with a plan to move their pirate into adulthood by setting limits, decreasing support, and providing a plan to help him grow up.

Thought for the Day

When you and your spouse create a comfortable life, your teen may choose to settle in and make himself at home. Let your teen know that the opportunity to live in comfort comes with a price.

Scripture for the Day

"For even when we were with you, we gave you this rule: 'If a man will not work, he shall not eat.' We hear that some among you are idle. They are not busy; they are busybodies. Such people we command and urge in the Lord Jesus Christ to settle down and earn the bread they eat." (2 Thessalonians 3:10-12)

No Opinion

Parents are famous for telling teens what they are about to say, saying it, and then saying what they just said. But Proverbs 18:2 says, "A fool...delights in airing his own opinions." No, you're not a fool, but you can feel like one if your child never accepts your opinions.

Are you a foolish parent? Instead of talking so much, try not sharing your opinion at all for one day. Just take a break and find out what your teen has to say for a change. You'll never understand your teenager—her wants, desires, and needs—if you insert your opinion into every conversation. So stop sharing and start listening. Wait to offer your viewpoint until she asks for your opinion. (That will probably happen about the time she needs some help.) You may be surprised how mature she can be when she knows you are listening and her opinion matters.

Thought for the Day

Most conversations are about connecting and communicating value, not simply exchanging information. People want to know their opinion matters. By listening, you can let your teen know you value her. She just might respond by asking your opinion after she's shared hers. That's the way to engage in a healthy conversation.

Scripture for the Day

"...a time to tear and a time to mend, a time to be silent and a time to speak..." (Ecclesiastes 3:7)

Imperfect Families

You can help your child through the process of realizing that you aren't perfect. Dad isn't Superman, and Mom isn't Wonder Woman. If you're like me, you're far from ideal! Admitting the truth won't destroy your child's concept of who you are as a parent or damage your relationship with him. In fact, it can bring you closer together. And it will probably affirm what he already knows anyway: Nobody's perfect!

When you're up front about your imperfections, you help your teen feel a little more comfortable in his own skin. His world is filled with voices that remind him every day how imperfect he is. You can teach him by example how to have a confident but realistic assessment of himself. Being imperfect is okay. In fact, when your teen sees you making it in life even though you're not perfect, he will have a good reason to believe he can make it too—without trying to attain to an ideal he'll never reach this side of heaven.

Scripture for the Day

"Do not think of yourself more highly than you ought, but rather think of yourself with sober judgment, in accordance with the measure of faith God has given you." (Romans 12:3)

Question for the Day

How do you handle your own imperfections? What does that communicate to your teen?

Rules and Relationships

Rules without relationship can cause rebellion in a teenager. Relationship without rules can cause chaos. How can you find the right balance?

First, when you develop your rules for your home, be clear about the goal: to bring your teenager safely to maturity. Second, when your rules are broken (and they will be), calmly enforce the appropriate consequences. And third, spend one-on-one time with your teen every week, doing something she likes to do, to help build your relationship.

These three principles are foundational to maintaining harmony, discipline, and strong relationships in your home. They will help you provide a healthy balance of rules and relationship so those two things work together, not against each other.

Thought for the Day

Your teen may outwardly balk at the mention of rules, but deep inside, she'll appreciate that your rules communicate what is good for everyone living in your home. She'll also appreciate that you care enough to set and enforce the rules.

Scripture for the Day

"I run in the path of your commands, for you have set my heart free." (Psalm 119:32)

Common Ground

When I tell people my wife and I have been through marriage counseling, they can relate. When they hear me say I don't always think straight, they know what I'm talking about. When I share that a board member of ours always tells people, "Mark is a lot smarter than he looks," people feel free to laugh at a face that's perfect for radio. And then they open up and tell me about their struggles—not because of my accomplishments or my line of work, but because I'm up front about my problems, my stupid mistakes, and the messes I've made. I share my "stuff" so that they'll be comfortable sharing theirs.

The same can be true for you and your teen. If you want him to talk about his problems or hurts, open up and talk about some of your own. When he sees you admit and overcome your struggles, you give him hope that he can do the same...with the encouragement of a parent who not only cares but also understands what he's going through.

Scripture for the Day

"If I must boast, I will boast of the things that show my weakness...I will boast all the more gladly about my weaknesses, so that Christ's power may rest on me...For when I am weak, then I am strong." (2 Corinthians 11:30; 12:9-10)

Question for the Day

Are you struggling or growing in a certain area? Can you talk about it with your teen?

Holding
Title

Teens today seem to feel entitled to things that aren't theirs and that they haven't earned. Parents are often generous with their young children, so when those kids become teens, they continue to believe that their parents owe them. Kids today are given so much by their parents and schools with no strings attached that they develop a false sense of being entitled to just about everything. That often leads to an insatiable appetite for more and more, and it can also tempt teens to not take care of what they already have.

When a wise parent gives something to his teenager, he finds a way to let the teen earn it somehow. And when kids earn something, and especially when they wait to receive it until they have earned it, they savor it more than if someone had simply handed it to them.

Thought for the Day

Sometimes parents give their children things because they need to feel appreciated and not simply because they love them.

Scripture for the Day

"Godliness with contentment is great gain." (1 Timothy 6:6)

Prayer for the Day

Lord, save me from trying to buy a relationship with my teen.

 # Adoption Void

Parents who adopt can give children better lives than they would have had otherwise. And the children often appreciate their adoptive parents and everything they have done for them. But quite naturally, in the teen years, kids question why their birth mothers gave them up. This is normal. When they begin thinking abstractly, they need to mentally process their adoption in entirely new ways.

Regardless of how much love they have received from their adoptive parents, adopted kids often experience this period of emotional turbulence. Parents can take advantage of this opportunity to connect with their adopted kids as they revisit this issue together. If your adopted teen is acting up today, this turmoil is likely the root cause. Help her through this transition, and rest assured that she will get to the other side.

Scripture for the Day

"Religion that God our Father accepts as pure and faultless is this: to look after orphans and widows in their distress and to keep oneself from being polluted by the world." (James 1:27)

Thought for the Day

Orphans can be distressed not only because of their living conditions but also because they feel abandoned.

The Blended Family

When two families are blended in marriage, relationships can become complicated. The role of stepparent can be the most difficult to fulfill, even when the stepparent is everything a teen would ever want in a parent.

The adjustment to a new living arrangement can be challenging, especially for teenagers, who often lose their privacy and their established place in the family. Blending families can ignite emotional upheaval because a new parent is a constant reminder of what the child has lost. A teen may intellectually understand that the new parent can never live up to the former parent, but emotionally, the teen may hold on to that fantasy. This can be confusing for the teen. So give kids time and space to honestly work through their feelings. Get them into counseling if they show signs of depression or self-harm. In the end, kids are resilient, and they will eventually come around.

Scripture for the Day

"The LORD gives strength to his people; the LORD blesses his people with peace." (Psalm 29:11)

Prayer for the Day

Lord, I'm trying to get things back in order, but everything appears to be out of order. Would You soften the hearts of everyone in my blended family? Help everyone feel hopeful about our new family unit.

Listen Slowly

A young lady once told her dad that she wanted to tell him something important—and she promised to tell him really fast! Fortunately, her dad picked up on what was happening and realized for the first time that his overly efficient (impatient) listening hindered his talkative princess from fully connecting with him. With a tear in his eye, he replied, "Honey, you can tell me all about it, and you don't have to tell me really fast. You can say it slowly. I'm here to listen."

Most of the time, your teen says things to you or to others not to communicate information but simply to process life. She doesn't need a response or a judgment, she doesn't need an opinion, and she probably isn't really asking for anything. She just needs a listening ear. So take time to listen—slowly.

Thought for the Day

Frankly, this is more often a problem for Dad than for Mom—but you can work on it as a team.

Scripture for the Day

"He will turn the hearts of the fathers to their children, and the hearts of the children to their fathers." (Malachi 4:6)

Prayer for the Day

Lord, help me listen better so I can hear things from my teen that I haven't heard before.

Strong-Willed

President Theodore Roosevelt said, "I can be president of the United States, or I can control my daughter, Alice. I cannot do both."

Parents of strong-willed kids understand that it takes a lot of time, attention, and effort to harness the energy of a strong-willed teen and put it to good use. There never seems to be a shortage of things to talk about when you have a teen always challenging the system with a strong willfulness. Strong-willed kids need clear boundaries and parents who are on the same discipline page. Clearly communicate your household boundaries and agree on consequences in advance. As your teen decides whether the "fun" he's considering is worth the consequences, he will learn how to harness his bullheadedness and rebellion and use that energy to become a competent, strong, principled young adult.

Thought for the Day

Kids who are strong willed, hyperactive, ADHD, or rebellious are often diamonds in the rough. During adolescence, their rough edges are smoothed out, and their beautiful personalities emerge.

Scripture for the Day

"When a country is rebellious, it has many rulers, but a man of understanding and knowledge maintains order." (Proverbs 28:2)

Money and Self-Control

The most important thing parents can teach their children is how to get along without them. Your teen will be independent someday. The question is, will she be ready when the time comes?

Preparing your child to be independent includes helping her learn how to manage money. I recommend giving kids a checkbook on their thirteenth birthday so they can learn how to wisely spend money for school, entertainment, and necessities. You think that's a crazy idea? Give it a chance. Most teens rise to the occasion and fulfill what is expected of them. Establish a budget and a schedule for deposits, but don't bail her out if she blows her lunch money on something else. If she spends unwisely, she needs to learn to work to replace the money or go without. And don't bail her out if she overspends or bounces a check. Let the learning process have its full effect. Learning responsibility in finances teaches your teen self-control, not only in spending, but in every aspect of life.

Scripture for the Day

"A student is not above his teacher, but everyone who is fully trained will be like his teacher." (Luke 6:40)

Thought for the Day

The number one topic of marital strife during the first year of marriage is finances. Save your future son- or daughter-in-law the pain of having to go through that difficult time.

Empathy

'm glad I'm not a teenager today. It's a tough, confusing, and constantly tempting world. I can only imagine what a mess I would be if I were growing up in this culture. So when teens get caught up in it and make wrong choices, let's not be too quick to judge them without first making an effort to understand their world. When you do, you'll gain a new appreciation for how difficult it can be, and that will temper the way you respond. Your anger may change to empathy.

Of course, poor choices still require appropriate consequences. But your appreciation of how difficult life can be for your teen will go a long way toward helping him learn from his mistakes. It will also help him not to get frustrated and not to get mad at you.

Scripture for the Day

"My son, preserve sound judgment and discernment, do not let them out of your sight; they will be life for you, an ornament to grace your neck. Then you will go on your way in safety, and your foot will not stumble; when you lie down, you will not be afraid; when you lie down, your sleep will be sweet. Have no fear of sudden disaster or of the ruin that overtakes the wicked, for the LORD will be your confidence and will keep your foot from being snared." (Proverbs 3:21-26)

Prayer for the Day

Lord, help me understand my teen's world so I may lay down my hostility and frustration and pick up understanding and empathy. Help me speak truth to him and offer light in his darkness.

Listening More

A Sunday school teacher once asked her ten-year-olds, "What's wrong with grown-ups?"

A boy responded, "Grown-ups never really listen because they already know what they're going to answer."

If this sounds like you, it may be time to admit that listening is not something you do well. Polishing up your listening skills is never a bad thing. Good listening habits can easily get tossed aside in the business of life. But the way you listen to your child goes a long way in determining his willingness to share his deep concerns with you. If you want him to know that his concerns are important to you, that your relationship with him is a priority for you, and that you're willing to give him your time, you'll need to convince him by the way you listen. So even when it's difficult to do so, practice just listening to your teen with plenty of eye contact and without preparing to answer.

Scripture for the Day

"He who answers before listening—that is his folly and his shame." (Proverbs 18:13)

Prayer for the Day

Heavenly Father, as I incline my ear to You, would You help me listen and be my hearing aid? Open my ears and bridle my tongue so I may hear my teen's heart. Help me listen in a way that lets him know he is safe with me and that I love him.

The High Bar of Life

My high school swimming coach suggested I join the track team during our off-season. He thought I might be a high jumper. He was a great swim coach, but he clearly didn't know much about track. The high jump was all wrong for someone my size. I couldn't clear the bar, so I became discouraged and quit the track team. He thought I was a failure, I thought he was an idiot, and we parted ways feeling disappointed with each other.

That lesson taught me not to set the high bar of life unrealistically high for a teenager and to consider whether my hopes for her line up with her gifts. A good life coach knows to start with the basics, to begin with the bar low enough to guarantee some success, and to build on each achievement. Over time you can raise the bar slightly as your teen develops life skills. But make sure you've matched the right opportunities with the right person so one of you doesn't look like a failure, the other doesn't look like an idiot, and you don't part ways.

Scripture for the Day

"All this is evidence that God's judgment is right, and as a result you will be counted worthy of the kingdom of God, for which you are suffering." (1 Timothy 1:5)

Thought for the Day

If your teen is frustrated, unmotivated, or giving up, perhaps the bar is too high. Or maybe your teen is working toward the wrong goal. Check your motives before your teen checks out.

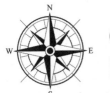

Getting Back in the Saddle

I often use horses in our Heartlight therapeutic program because many life lessons can be gained from learning how to ride a horse. When kids get on a horse for the first time, chances are they will fall off. When that happens, we don't criticize their skills; we encourage them to get back on. They may fall off yet again, so we encourage them to get on again. And we compliment them for their courage when they get back up in the saddle. During this process, the horse doesn't usually change, but the rider eventually learns how to better manage the horse and overcome his own awkwardness and fear. Likewise, when your teenager falls off track in life, you can encourage him to get back on. He'll probably fall again, and you can help him back up again. Your encouragement (not your criticism) will make all the difference.

Scripture for the Day

"Therefore encourage one another and build each other up, just as in fact you are doing." (1 Thessalonians 5:11)

Thought for the Day

When you're tempted to say, "I told you so," try encouraging instead. Rather than pointing out what your teen can't do, help him see what he can.

Prayer for the Day

Encourage me, Lord, and help me to always encourage my teen.

Enabling Responsibility

A mom and dad were upset because their daughter didn't mail her college application on time. I had recommended that they let her be responsible to follow through. She didn't, and she learned a difficult lesson as a result. Her parents didn't get what they wanted, but she sure got what she needed—a lesson that she could learn only by making a mistake and assuming full responsibility.

You are a facilitator for your teen, not a doer. Support her, but make sure she knows you won't pick up the ball and run with it for her all the time. As she gets older, spend more time passing the ball to her rather than always running it yourself. She needs to learn to handle the important things in life, and she will never learn until she drops the ball a few times. So keep this in mind: The earlier a lesson is learned, the less critical the consequences will be.

Scripture for the Day

"We also rejoice in our sufferings, because we know that suffering produces perseverance; perseverance, character; and character, hope. And hope does not disappoint us, because God has poured out his love into our hearts by the Holy Spirit, whom he has given us." (Romans 5:3-5)

Prayer for the Day

Lord, help me to not hog the ball so much, but rather to pass it to my teen more often so she can learn not to fumble in life. Show me ways to teach her how to get in the game.

What You Can Do and What You Can't

You can teach your teen, but learning the lesson is up to him. You can give him advice, but he must choose whether he will accept it. And you can be a spiritual leader in your home, but he will decide for himself what he believes.

Some young adults need to explore their options before they are ready to return to their spiritual roots. I've heard people say that a child has to give up his parents' faith so he can embrace his own. If your child has given up yours, he may be in the process of embracing his. This could be a time of transition—and transitions are rarely easy.

Instead of weakening your relationship by frowning on his behavior and decisions, keep praying and accepting him as he is. Try loving him into the kingdom. After all, there's only so much you can do.

Scripture for the Day

"See that you do not look down on one of these little ones. For I tell you that their angels in heaven always see the face of my Father in heaven." (Matthew 18:10-11)

Thought for the Day

I have always been eager to save the lost, but I didn't always notice and pay attention to the lost one in my own home. Do you?

Growing Wisdom

Your teen's growth in wisdom and self-reliance begins with you! You are the one who increases her levels of responsibility as she gets older and prepares to leave home. As she succeeds in her newfound decision-making role, add more responsibility, helping her to step up again and again and again. This process will eventually lead her from being an immature, dependent child to being a responsible adult who can handle things on her own.

If you take one step at a time and offer plenty of encouragement and incentives (such as more freedom), your teen will enjoy stepping up to meet the new demands.

Scripture for the Day

"The fear of the Lord is the beginning of knowledge, but fools despise wisdom and discipline." (Proverbs 1:7)

Thought for the Day

Teens mature as they assume responsibility. They learn to value good decisions by making their own choices. They appreciate wisdom when they experience the results of their foolishness.

Question for the Day

What new level of responsibility can you help your teen step up to in her journey toward maturity?

Sparks

A man once told me of his lifelong struggle with low self-esteem. A grade school teacher once told him, "You'd be smart if you had as much brains as you do fat." He was 42 years old when he told me the story, but it still brought a tear to his eye.

Critical comments like this can create a lifelong tear in the fabric of a child's self-esteem.

Ask your teen today if you have ever said reckless words to him in a moment of harsh criticism or thoughtlessness. He might remember something you've forgotten. If so, ask for his forgiveness, and your relationship will begin to heal. And more importantly, you will prevent a lifetime of anger and hurt because of words you don't even remember saying. "Sticks and stones may break my bones, but words will never hurt me?" Ha! That's a myth.

Scripture for the Day

"Reckless words pierce like a sword, but the tongue of the wise brings healing." (Proverbs 12:18)

Thought for the Day

Regardless of what you intend to say, the hearer's perception is his truth. We should act upon that.

Prayer for the Day

Lord, help me to choose my words carefully and to ask for forgiveness for my reckless words.

Ask and Rest

Your teen faces an incredible amount of stress today, so make your home a place where she can find peace, encouragement, and unconditional love. Let it be a retreat from the pressures of life, a refuge where her soul can find rest.

Do you know if your home is a restful place for your teen? Have you asked her? She'll tell you. And if her answer isn't what you hoped to hear, don't get defensive. Work together to come up with some ways to make positive changes. Remember, if your teen cannot find rest and acceptance in your home, she'll seek it in other places—good or bad.

Scripture for the Day

"Some became fools through their rebellious ways and suffered affliction because of their iniquities...Then they cried to the LORD in their trouble, and he saved them from their distress. He sent forth his word and healed them; he rescued them from the grave. Let them give thanks to the LORD for his unfailing love and his wonderful deeds for men." (Psalm 107:17-21)

Thought for the Day

If your teen is involved in inappropriate behavior, she probably won't want to be at home, where she might be exposed. Or maybe she hasn't done anything wrong, but you have. Asking how you can create a better environment for her can be a wonderful way to let her know that you want your home to be a place of rest.

Asking Questions

Do your parents know everything that happened to you when you were a teenager? Probably not.

Recently a high school sophomore told me he had an affair with his teacher. His parents were shocked to find out (of course) and asked their son why he hadn't told them. He responded, "You never asked." Parents often assume their teen will tell them if something inappropriate is happening in his life. Usually the opposite is true— he'll be too ashamed and embarrassed to say anything. But if you ask him directly and without accusation, he will likely open up. So be wise and ask important questions, especially if your teen's mood or behavior suddenly changes.

Scripture for the Day

"Ask and it will be given to you; seek and you will find; knock and the door will be opened to you. For everyone who asks receives; he who seeks finds; and to him who knocks, the door will be opened." (Matthew 7:7-8)

Thought for the Day

Get into the habit of asking questions more and sharing your opinion less. It's not that your opinion doesn't matter; you just might not have the full story.

Prayer for the Day

Lord, help me ask questions that touch my teen's heart and stimulate his thoughts.

Bad Company

Is your teen being influenced by bad company?

When problems first arise with a teenager, many parents make the mistake of blaming the teen's friends for causing their "angelic" child to take a walk on the dark side. After all, "bad company corrupts good character," right? But I've found that teens seek out peers who think and act just like they do. In their distress, they want to find the comfort of others. It's like this. If I go into a Walmart at two a.m. in East Texas, chances are I will walk out feeling a lot better about my health, my appearance, and my social habits. The same is true for your teen.

So a wise parent will focus on his own teen and not shift blame to peer influences. Appropriate behavior is enforced by clear boundaries and consistent consequences, such as the loss of certain freedoms and privileges. The disciplined teen will eventually grow weary of hanging around with the wrong crowd and seek out others who think differently.

Scripture for the Day

"The tax collectors and 'sinners' were all gathering around to hear him. But the Pharisees and the teachers of the law muttered, 'This man welcomes sinners and eats with them.'" (Luke 15:1-2)

Thought for the Day

Rather than running from kids in need, you can run toward them. Invite a few kids over for a movie night or include them on your next family outing. They may need someone like you.

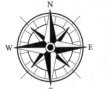

Rooted in Loss

Did you know that losses in a teen's life can trigger behavioral problems? These losses may be traumatic, like the death of a parent, divorce, or the loss of innocence and self-respect. Others are subtler, like the loss of friends when moving to a new home or the death of a pet. These losses can trigger all sorts of inappropriate teen behavior. Your teen may not even know why she's acting out, so if you can, help her identify the reason she feels the way she does. Your understanding of the real issue will flavor and soften your approach toward your teen's behavior. And eventually, your teen will learn to handle loss in more appropriate ways and perhaps realize that Christ Himself can fill those voids in everyone's life.

Scripture for the Day

"Therefore, since we have a great high priest who has gone through the heavens, Jesus the Son of God, let us hold firmly to the faith we profess. For we do not have a high priest who is unable to sympathize with our weaknesses, but we have one who has been tempted in every way, just as we are—yet was without sin." (Hebrews 4:14-16)

Thought for the Day

Focusing only on the glass that is half full provides an optimistic outlook on life. But sometimes you need to look at the half empty part so God can fill those voids in your life. Then you won't be controlled by what you don't have or what you have lost. Rather, you'll be motivated by what you do have—His fullness. And you can help your teen walk through the same process.

Higher Priorities

Parents of teens need a double dose of wisdom to know what is a big deal and what isn't. We can easily major on the minors and make mountains out of molehills. But if we leave some of those issues alone, they will eventually pass on their own. For example, is a teen's messy room going to keep him out of heaven? Is his unkempt hair and untucked shirt as important as the condition of his heart? There are bigger issues in life that require open communication, so don't create a blockage by constantly nagging about trivial matters. Does your teen avoid family gathering times because he's afraid of being lectured about some small issue? Might he have something more important to talk about?

Have regular discussions about what seems to be important for right now. Your teen needs to hear what you think is important, and vice versa. Hash it out with your teen, and you'll ensure that you're focusing on what is important.

Scripture for the Day

"Aim for perfection, listen to my appeal, be of one mind, live in peace. And the God of love and peace will be with you." (2 Corinthians 13:11)

Prayer for the Day

Lord, help me attend to the important things, let the unimportant things go, and show my teen how to distinguish between the two.

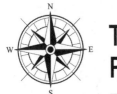

Truthful Parenting

Does telling your teenager the truth sometimes seem harsh? A father once asked a counselor what to tell his two teenagers after their mother abandoned the family. The counselor immediately replied, "Don't lie; tell your children the truth. Protect their mother's reputation as much as possible, but tell them what's happened, and do it immediately. Your children will always remember your honesty, and in the long run, they'll thank you for it."

That was good advice. Your teenager expects you to always tell her the truth, regardless of how much it hurts. The quickest way to lose your teen's respect is to not be honest with her. Make a habit of telling "the truth, the whole truth, and nothing but the truth." Sowing seeds of truthfulness will reap a great harvest, especially when you need to hear the truth from her.

Scripture for the Day

"Do not lie to each other, since you have taken off your old self with its practices and have put on the new self, which is being renewed in knowledge in the image of its Creator." (Colossians 3:9-10)

Prayer for the Day

Lord, may my mouth always be a fountain of truth. Help me to share the truth, the whole truth, and nothing but the truth...even when doing so is difficult.

Keep Quiet

C an you remember the last time your teen asked for your opinion about something? If it's been a long time, perhaps you offer it a little too freely instead of really listening to what she has to say.

If your conversations have been too one-sided in the past, you can help rebuild communication with your teen by finding an activity she enjoys and participating in it together. Then just keep quiet. Create space for her to talk rather than filling all the silence. Quietness invites discussion, and it shows her that you're confident she can engage with you and even carry the conversation.

Does silence make you nervous? Your teen feels the same way. Let her fill it. Talking less during an activity may be difficult, but when it comes to getting teenagers to open up, you can't be too quiet, even if you don't say anything the whole time! So find opportunities to communicate, but turn the tables. Instead of leading the discussion, let your teenager do the talking.

Scripture for the Day

"He who guards his lips guards his life, but he who speaks rashly will come to ruin." (Proverbs 13:3)

Prayer for the Day

Lord, I know that loose lips sink ships, so help me keep silent at times with my teen. Help me enjoy the silence and use it as an opportunity to hear Your voice of direction.

Learning the
Hard Way

If your older teen is not responding to your rules and discipline and is bringing danger to your family, you may have only two choices left: You can let him stay at home and continue to wreak havoc within your family, or you can ask him to leave. This is a difficult and painful decision, but parents shouldn't allow one prodigal (who is legally an adult) to destroy the good things going for the rest of the family. Provision for an older teen can quickly move into enabling.

Sometimes older teens learn best on their own from the school of hard knocks while the parents pray that God will teach them what they've been unable to learn at home. Of course, you can always leave the door open for the older teen to return home when he demonstrates that he can function within the boundaries you have determined.

Scripture for the Day

"As for you, brothers, never tire of doing what is right. If anyone does not obey our instruction in this letter, take special note of him. Do not associate with him, in order that he may feel ashamed. Yet do not regard him as an enemy, but warn him as a brother." (2 Thessalonians 3:13-15)

Thought for the Day

If the tack you're taking with your teen isn't working now, it's not likely to be more effective later. This might be the time for a change.

Freedom
of Choice

Life is all about choices, and your teenager may make the wrong ones more often than not. If she never chooses wrong, she'll never experience the consequences that provide the negative reinforcement for everything you have taught her. On the other hand, her wrong choices will usually confirm and validate the need to choose wisely. So let her make some choices of her own.

Just as I believe in the gospel, the authority of Scripture, and the deity of Christ, I also believe in the freedom of choice. Besides, when an older teen chooses something that moves her in the wrong direction, you can't always do something about it. And even when you can, your answers (and mine) can fall short. In these situations, trust God to do whatever is necessary to move your teen to a better place than where you could lead her on her own.

Scripture for the Day

"Some trust in chariots and some in horses, but we trust in the name of the LORD our God." (Psalm 20:7)

Question for the Day

Is it difficult for you to let your teen make her own decisions? Why is that so hard? Do you have a need to be in control? Are you able to trust God to watch over, protect, and guide her?

Responsible Remembering

Is your teen conveniently forgetful? He may need to work on ways to remember what you ask him to do, but the real problem is more likely to be that he's slacking off in his responsibilities. Forgetting is sometimes a way to deal with feeling a bit intimidated by what you've asked him to do. Or he may not be able to finish a task in the time frame you asked. So instead, he just ignores you.

Don't allow him to shirk his responsibilities by forgetting. Tell him that remembering is his responsibility, as is completing the task. Put a note on the refrigerator (just one), send a text (but don't nag), or put up a chalkboard titled "Chores for Today" (a small one) to help him remember. He has a lot on his plate, and he may sometimes forget just because he's an adolescent, but don't let that be an excuse for irresponsibility. And let the consequences of forgetting teach him how to remember better the next time. He will be better off if he learns the importance of remembering now than if he waits until he's on a job or in a marriage.

Scripture for the Day

"Get wisdom, get understanding; do not forget my words or swerve from them." (Proverbs 4:5)

Prayer for the Day

Lord, remind me to remind my teen to be more responsible in his remembering...to remember the things he's learned from me and from You.

Grace and Consequences

How does a parent show grace to a child? Certainly not by going easy, eliminating consequences, or trying to act more like a friend than a parent. Parents who resort to these behaviors are usually (though not consciously) more concerned about meeting their own needs than their teens'.

One troubled teen used her mom's divorce as an excuse to act out inappropriately any time she pleased. The mom felt too guilty about the divorce to correct her teen, who took advantage of the situation. The mom wasn't really offering grace; she was giving license. She wasn't helping her teen; she was hurting. As a result, the teen's mean and obnoxious ways continued into adulthood.

A parent shows grace to her child by holding her accountable while at the same time standing by her as she suffers the consequences, just as God stands by you.

Scripture for the Day

"You, my brothers, were called to be free. But do not use your freedom to indulge the sinful nature; rather, serve one another in love." (Galatians 5:13)

Prayer for the Day

Lord, You are the ultimate giver of grace. Would You help me think like You do and treat my teen the way You treat me?

Preparation and Training

The admonition in Proverbs 22:6 to train our children has both spiritual and practical implications. If we focus only on our teens' spiritual development, we may neglect to train them in areas where they put spiritual precepts into practice. We must teach teens how to navigate society with their faith and integrity intact, but we should also teach them how to handle money, work, clean, cook, and shop. This is not the schools' job. Home is where our teens learn about financial responsibility, credit card debt, building a future, and developing relationships. Home is where their work ethic and godly character are shaped. So it is up to you, Mom and Dad, to train your teen to do more for himself. When he is older, he'll thank you for the way you prepared him practically as well as spiritually.

Scripture for the Day

"Make it your ambition to lead a quiet life, to mind your own business and to work with your hands, just as we told you, so that your daily life may win the respect of outsiders and so that you will not be dependent on anybody." (1 Thessalonians 4:11-12)

Thought for the Day

If we teach our teens how to be competent in many ways, perhaps they will go on to honor and serve one another and God in ways we would have never dreamed. Training may be hard work, but the results will probably far outweigh the costs.

Tattoo Grace

Sometimes wise parents do things they never imagined in order to demonstrate unconditional love to their children. One wise friend of ours has a nineteen-year-old daughter who wanted a small heart-shaped tattoo on her ankle. Like most parents, the mother didn't like tattoos and never dreamed of allowing her daughter to get one. But instead of refusing, she decided not only to go with her daughter (who was going regardless of what Mom said) but also to get an identical tattoo on her own ankle! Sharing the pain and permanence of a matching tattoo demonstrated her love for her daughter and went a long way toward healing a breach in their relationship.

You show grace when you give your teen something she doesn't deserve, but you can also show grace by stepping outside your world to be with your teen in hers.

Question for the Day

I'm not suggesting you get a tattoo with your teen. But how can you go the extra mile today to demonstrate your love for your teenager and your commitment to your relationship with her?

Prayer for the Day

Lord, I admit that I don't like stepping outside my comfort zone. But I am willing to dream with You, Lord...how would You have me demonstrate my love for my teen and my commitment to our relationship? Help me to be sensitive to Your creative leading, and give me strength to act when the opportunity arises.

Yanking His Chain

If you treat your teenager like a child, you will most likely get childish behavior in return. If you treat him like a stubborn mule, yanking and pulling him toward mature thinking, he will only yank all the harder the other way. So instead, create an atmosphere that encourages your teen to move in the right direction, granting small increases in freedom as rewards for making good decisions. A teenager is a young adult and wants to begin making his own decisions just as you and I do. Respect his decision making as you would any other adult's, and he'll begin showing signs of adult-like behavior in return.

Scripture for the Day

"I will instruct you and teach you in the way you should go; I will counsel you and watch over you. Do not be like the horse or the mule, which have no understanding but must be controlled by bit and bridle or they will not come to you." (Psalm 32:8-9)

Thought for the Day

I ask young people not to shoot the messenger (that would be me). Staying calm, listening patiently, and conversing as adults helps them develop wisdom, take responsibility for their lives, and stop shifting blame and making excuses.

Question for the Day

In what way can you treat your teen like an adult and encourage him to respond like one?

Defining Fences

One of my weekend chores at the Heartlight ranch is to repair the fences. I enjoy time out in the field digging holes, pounding posts, and stretching wire. It's hard, tiresome work, but I never have to worry that the horses are going to wander off or get out of line.

Just as fences help our horses, personal boundaries help your teenager. They keep her safe and help her know what is good for her until she can think more clearly and maturely on her own. Until she has the internal controls she needs to succeed in her world, you'll probably have to keep establishing and reinforcing reasonable boundaries, just as I keep tending the fences at Heartlight. When you stay on top of those external controls, you can rest assured that she's not going to wander off or get out of line.

Scripture for the Day

"Like a city whose walls are broken down is a man who lacks self-control." (Proverbs 25:28)

Thought for the Day

Within those fences that I maintain, the horses are free to do as they please. They enjoy the security of the fences and relish their freedom to run, eat, roll, and generally act like horses. I can provide a wonderful environment for them simply by maintaining the fences.

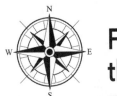 # Fuel on the Flames

The way you respond to your teenager's occasional mess ups is critically important. Even when you intend to calm a situation, your teen may feel as if you are throwing fuel on a fire. If you get angry when your teen does something wrong, here's my advice: Allow the consequences to do the teaching, not your anger. Reasonable consequences will build maturity in your teen, but anger will build resentment and short-circuit what he may have learned from his mistake.

You can defuse your anger by recalling your own teenage mistakes. When you're cooled down, you can deal with your teen's mistake and apply the consequences more effectively. Remember, your approach helps determine the type of reaction or response you'll get in return. Approach him calmly and gently. Someday, both of you will be able to laugh at your silly teenage stunts.

Scripture for the Day

"A wise man fears the LORD and shuns evil, but a fool is hotheaded and reckless." (Proverbs 14:16)

Question for the Day

How do you normally respond to bad news about your teen's behavior? Do you tend to add fuel to the fire, or do you extinguish the flames? How can you improve your approach and encourage a calm response?

A Greater Gift

At our Heartlight counseling center, I work every day with teens who have hit rock bottom. These are all great kids—no different from yours or mine—but they have experienced some tough times because of difficult circumstances, poor parenting, or their own unwise choices.

You may be surprised to learn that some of the despair I find in these teens is a by-product of receiving too much from their parents, not too little. Overindulgence makes a teen feel entitled to more and more. Giving her everything motivates her for nothing. So hold back on giving too much to your teen, and give her the satisfaction of working for what she owns. Sometimes the greater gift is to give her less.

Scripture for the Day

"The sluggard craves and gets nothing, but the desires of the diligent are fully satisfied." (Proverbs 13:4)

Thought for the Day

You may have received very little when you were young and have a desire to provide good things for your teen. But be careful. You might be motivated to give to accommodate your own sense of loss. That would mean your giving is more about you than it is about your teen. This is a dangerous path to follow.

Shunned and Shamed

Some parents shun teens whose lifestyle is different from theirs. They may shame teens who make choices against a mother's or father's greater wisdom. These parents evidently believe that breaking the relationship will encourage the child to return to the parents' values. From my experience, it won't!

Sadly, many go to the grave thinking they were justified in treating an errant child like a disease instead of embracing him with godly love and grace. Here's my advice. When your child reaches adulthood, set aside your correctional role and accept him as a valid and loved member of the family regardless of the choices he makes. You don't have to accept his lifestyle, ignore your boundaries, or bend the rules of your home to accommodate him. You can extend your hand in relationship without supporting him in his lifestyle. He is still your teen, and you may be the only beacon that can lead him home.

Scripture for the Day

"I tell you who hear me: Love your enemies, do good to those who hate you, bless those who curse you, pray for those who mistreat you. If someone strikes you on one cheek, turn to him the other also. If someone takes your cloak, do not stop him from taking your tunic. Give to everyone who asks you, and if anyone takes what belongs to you, do not demand it back. Do to others as you would have them do to you...Love your enemies, do good to them, and lend to them without expecting to get anything back." (Luke 6:27-31, 35)

Unconditional Love

A healthy relationship with your teen is founded on unconditional love—a love that never ends. It doesn't stop when your child doesn't respond the way she should, or when she makes a mistake, or even when she stops loving you. Some parents base their love on performance or good behavior. We can be thankful God doesn't love us that way. If He did, we'd all be in trouble.

Just as we are secure in our salvation, teens gain stability and security when their relationships with their parents aren't conditional. So model God's love today in the way you parent your teen, and she will better understand God's eternal gift of life to us.

Scripture for the Day

"We love because he first loved us." (1 John 4:19)

Thought for the Day

Loving your child is easy when all is going well. But can you love her when she disappoints you, openly rebels against you, and blatantly disregards what she knows is true? That's when she needs you the most.

Prayer for the Day

Father, You are always building on my relationship with You, even when I'm experiencing Your discipline. Help me to consistently build on my relationship with my teen.

When Your Teen Rejects You

Does your teenager go out of his way to avoid family dinners, spend all his time in his room, shut down when you speak to him, or refuse to spend any time with your family? Does he say he hates your family even though he used to love you? If your teen suddenly refuses to spend time with your family, or if he is always with new friends and never with you—and especially if he has a disrespectful or hateful attitude—your teen may be on the verge of spinning out of control.

A little intolerance for parents or family is normal in every teen's life. But when your teen constantly rejects your family, it's time to investigate, take a deeper look into his life, and seek wise counsel about what to do.

Scripture for the Day

"We have spoken freely to you...and opened wide our hearts to you. We are not withholding our affection from you, but you are withholding yours from us. As a fair exchange—I speak as to my children—open wide your hearts also." (2 Corinthians 6:11-13)

Thought for the Day

All behavior is goal oriented, so search for the issues driving your teen's behavior. He may be isolating himself because of guilt, shame, embarrassment, or some other kind of pain. He may have experienced something you don't know about. Create a safe environment for him, and continue asking, continue looking, and continue being available.

Reward Your Teen

A good way to help your teen learn to behave responsibly is to affirm her, praise her progress, and reward her. Encouraging your teen when she makes good decisions will go a long way toward helping her continue to make wise choices. So when she gets it right, celebrate! Applaud! Be sincere, but make a big deal out of it, even if your teen thinks you're being corny.

Focus your attention on her successes, not her failures. Patiently give her more and more opportunities to make right choices, and keep on the lookout for progress. Whenever you see your child respond with maturity and responsibility, congratulate her and move her up to a new level of freedom as a reward. And keep in mind that instant feedback is always best. A good word at a good time has an amazing way of making for a good relationship.

Scripture for the Day

"Bless those who persecute you; bless and do not curse. Rejoice with those who rejoice; mourn with those who mourn." (Romans 12:14-15)

Thought for the Day

If correcting your teen's inappropriate behavior more and more isn't helping her make better choices, try rewarding her appropriate behavior. Recognize her progress instead of always drawing attention to her failures. Affirming the good may eventually eliminate the bad.

Satisfy the Faint

Being a teenager isn't easy. Your teen's body is changing, his world is growing and becoming less controlled, his choices are increasing and carrying greater consequences...and he has never felt more alone. This can be a tough time for your teen, and he can grow weary. When he does, you can respond to him the same way God responds to you: "I will refresh the weary and satisfy the faint" (Jeremiah 31:25).

To help your teen adapt to these challenges, adapt your style of parenting. Find ways to make your home a place of rest for your teen. As you lecture less and listen more, you can help your teen feel refreshed, restored, and confident in his ability to overcome obstacles and succeed.

Thought for the Day

Consider how many of your words to your teen could be categorized as "encouraging" and how many could be considered "correcting." Put yourself in his shoes and replay your conversations from his perspective. Think of ways you can improve your listening skills so he feels freer to talk with you.

Question for the Day

Is your home a place of conflict or a place of rest? Does your teen feel more burdened after a discussion with you or less burdened? Does your teen smile or frown when he catches a glimpse of you?

Adoption Wisdom

Adoptive parents are often unprepared for the unexpected barrage of identity problems that may surface when an adopted child becomes a teen. Jan and I have counseled hundreds of bewildered and broken adoptive parents who never expected their adopted teens to have such intense and unhappy struggles to find their identities. You may have the disheartening feeling that all you've done for your child is going down the drain after years of a good relationship.

Loving and nurturing your child does not always prevent her from wanting to know why her mom gave her away. Many parents wonder, *How can something so well intended go so wrong?* But God knew your child would be likely to struggle with her identity, and He knew you would be able to help her through this time. If your adopted child has not yet entered this difficult season, be confident, be prepared...and don't be surprised when she does.

Scripture for the Day

"May our Lord Jesus Christ himself and God our Father, who loved us and by his grace gave us eternal encouragement and good hope, encourage your hearts and strengthen you in every good deed and word." (2 Thessalonians 2:16-17)

Prayer for the Day

Lord, You have adopted me and given me a new identity. Empower me to help my teen feel secure in her identity, just as You help me feel secure in mine.

Letting Go

This generation of parents has done a wonderful job of building relationships with their teens, but few parents of teens have planned for the process of letting go. Sometimes teens have a good reason to distance themselves from their parents—they're trying to find room to make their own decisions about their friends, activities, job, education, and marriage.

Instead of continuing to manage your teen the way you did when he was younger, come up with a plan for letting go, share it with him, and implement it. Having a full quiver of kids is great, and putting these "arrows" in the bow and launching them into new adventures in life can be even better. The tough part is letting go so they can fly, but you've got to do it. Sometimes a rebellious teen is really just trying to gain some independence from overprotective parents.

Scripture for the Day

"For this reason a man will leave his father and mother and be united to his wife, and they will become one flesh." (Genesis 2:24)

Thought for the Day

Your process of letting go will be better for you and for your teen if you prepare for it.

Prayer for the Day

Lord, help me let go so that my child can grab onto his next phase of life.

Zoo or Jungle

Too many teens today are raised to live in a zoo instead of being prepared to survive in a jungle.

You can't eliminate every bad influence that touches your teen's life. In fact, if you try, your child will stumble when she engages with her culture. Christian teens today are growing up in a post-Christian world filled with obstacles and pitfalls that can easily trip them up. But many of those teens have been so protected that they are unaware of the dangers of the real world or don't know how to respond to them. Instead of always protecting your teen, prepare her to live in the jungle. She can't (and shouldn't) run away from her culture or avoid it, so she needs you to prepare her to interact with it in a healthy way. That will never happen if you keep her in the zoo.

Scripture for the Day

"If you belonged to the world, it would love you as its own. As it is, you do not belong to the world, but I have chosen you out of the world. That is why the world hates you." (John 15:19)

Thought for the Day

The world can be a tough place and very different from the world we might wish existed. To think that we parents will always be there to protect our teens is unrealistic. Instead, let's get real about what the real world is like and let them practice applying the things we have taught them. When they stumble—and they will—we can provide a safe place for them to regroup.

Rules and Rulers

Have you established rules in your home, or do you act like a ruler your home? Have you considered the difference between the two?

Rules and proper boundaries help your teenager mature into a confident adult. But living under the authority of a parent who acts like a ruler can lead to frustration, rebellion, and eroded self-esteem. Old, worn-out platitudes like "Because I said so," "I don't care what you think," "It's my way or the highway," or "Do as I say, not as I do" are never helpful. If you continue to act like a ruler when your child becomes a teenager, you might get the chores done around your home, but you probably won't build a good relationship with her. Let your teen make more decisions on her own. Teenagers learn best from consequences, and you can help her by letting the consequences do their work when she chooses to break the household rules.

Scripture for the Day

"But you are not to be like that. Instead, the greatest among you should be like the youngest, and the one who rules like the one who serves." (Luke 22:26)

Prayer for the Day

Lord, help me give up control so that my teen can learn to exercise self-control. Letting go is difficult for me, so help me loosen my grip.

Teen Trouble

When your teen shares some bad news, consider taking a deep breath to ease the tension, affirming your teen with compassion and understanding, and when you respond, flavoring your words with wisdom and even some wit.

Today's culture creates unprecedented pressure and difficulties for your teen—and for you! So when bad news comes, you would do well to take a moment before you respond. Gather your thoughts, rein in your anger, and if needed, seek the counsel of someone you trust before you respond. Wait until the heat of the moment has cooled down. The way you respond could determine how the situation will turn out for you and your teen.

Making a helpful response to bad news isn't easy, but you can do it if you plan ahead.

Scripture for the Day

"Consider it pure joy, my brothers, whenever you face trials of many kinds, because you know that the testing of your faith develops perseverance." (James 1:2-3)

Thought for the Day

For years, I have lived with 50 teens on a regular basis. I've learned not to react immediately to anything and not to respond until 24 hours have passed. This tactic keeps me focused, and I find I usually handle things better than if I had responded sooner.

Teen Porn

The Internet is a wonderful tool. It has opened up a world of new information, communication, and business. But the downside of the Internet is the instant access to pornography—the Internet's most prolific and profitable industry. Your teen's generation is the first to have porn so readily available, so explicit, and so culturally accepted. And now teens can easily upload inappropriate pictures of themselves into the porn stream.

The digital age and the teen culture have combined to produce one of the most seductive and exposed generations in history. Pornography is so readily available and so popular that many teens now consider it normal. This accessibility and acceptance has turned every computer or phone into a potential *Playboy* magazine. Your child's conscience and reputation could be scarred for life, so dedicate yourself to monitoring your teen's Internet use.

Scripture for the Day

"I made a covenant with my eyes not to look lustfully at a girl." (Job 31:1)

Thought for the Day

I know very few young men who wouldn't "take a peek" if they had an opportunity. Guys are wired that way, but that doesn't excuse their behavior. You can't always be there to help your teen make the right decision, but you can help him by making sure that porn is not available in your home and by letting him know that you are monitoring his Internet use.

Teen Communications

Hiding the cracks in your own life is next to impossible when a teenager is in your home. They're as plain to her as the nose on your face. Try as you might, you simply cannot live a perfect life, and no one sees your imperfections more clearly than your highly sensitive teenager.

So quit trying to hide your mistakes. Take time to talk with your teenager about your struggles and your daily reliance on the grace of God. She will appreciate your honesty, and she will feel better about you and your failures when she knows you're aware of them and working on them. When you are up-front about your own weaknesses, you build a stronger bridge of truthfulness and openness with your teen, and you demonstrate for her a healthy way to deal with her own shortcomings now and as an adult.

Thought for the Day

Children may believe that they are supposed to be perfect or that their parents are perfect. Wise parents help their children understand that nobody is perfect—and that's okay. With this new perception, kids will feel more comfortable in their own skin, they will be saved from trying to reach an unattainable goal, and they will quickly realize their need for Christ.

Prayer for the Day

Heavenly Father, thank You for loving me even though I am far from perfect. Help me to be honest with my teen about my imperfections and to grow more like You every day. Thank You for using her to keep me honest, and please help her know how to live with her own imperfections.

Time-Wise Parenting

Parenting can seem easier in the earlier years, when kids think and act in more simple and concrete ways. So some parents have a rude awakening when the teen years come around. As kids approach this age, they begin to think more abstractly. Their worlds expand in every way, and they often don't know what to do with their newfound emotions and need for independence.

The best way for you to help your child through these changes in his thinking and feelings is to spend one-on-one time with him. Take time this week to let him talk about what's happening in his life. Make it a priority to link up with him now, regardless of what else is going on in your life or his life, and you'll avoid a crisis later.

Scripture for the Day

"Solid food is for the mature, who by constant use have trained themselves to distinguish good from evil." (Hebrews 5:14)

Thought for the Day

Your words may shape your teen's life somewhat, but your time and attention are much more important and powerful. He'll probably forget most of what you say, but he'll never forget that you were there for him.

Question for the Day

Do you spend more or less time with your child than you did before he entered adolescence?

The Disguise of Rebellion

No parent thinks, *Today I would really like my child to get frustrated and angry with me,* or *I really want my child to spin out of control and act rebellious.* But you can actually cause those things by responding inappropriately when your teen appears to be rebelling. Stay calm, focus on keeping your relationship intact, and find out what's on your teen's heart. Is she reacting to a situation you don't know about? Let your compassion for her and your understanding of her difficult situation temper your anger as you work together on the real problem.

I don't meet many rebellious teens. More than 2500 kids in crisis have lived with me. They're certainly not bad kids, and only a few were actually rebellious. Most, if not all, were merely responding to extremely challenging circumstances. Their responses are almost always entirely understandable, even though they are inappropriate. Take time to get to the heart of the matter, and you can change the heart of your teen.

Scripture for the Day

"Do not be quickly provoked in your spirit, for anger resides in the lap of fools." (Ecclesiastes 7:9)

Thought for the Day

Small problems can turn into bigger problems if you don't catch them early. When you focus only on your teen's behavior and not her troubled heart, you could be accidentally ignoring the real issues and allowing them to become more serious.

Tough Times for Teens

Scripture encourages me to look at life with the eyes of my heart, but I tend to look at things with the eyes on my face. If you're like me, you can easily get so focused on problems that you forget to consider the complete picture of what your teen needs amid his struggle. Remember, his behavior is *an* issue, but it's not *the* issue.

In your eagerness to help your teen through a tough time, don't forget to take a step back, consider the confused condition most teens are in these days, and offer your teen rest and refreshment instead of quick answers. If I spent all my time focusing on the problems of the teens that live with me, I would never have the time to develop deeper relationships with them and help them through their problems. Take the time to build that deeper relationship with your teen, and examine his problems with not only the eyes in your head but also the eyes of your heart.

Scripture for the Day

"I pray also that the eyes of your heart may be enlightened in order that you may know the hope to which he has called you, the riches of his glorious inheritance in the saints, and his incomparably great power for us who believe." (Ephesians 1:18-19)

Prayer for the Day

Lord, help me see beyond my teen's actions and into his heart, his head, and his longings so that I might offer him hope, significance, and a future.

Bad
News

If you ever get news that your teenager has done something really bad, let me assure you—God will help you get through it. I've seen God change what looked like the worst situation into a wonderful opportunity. You may experience a little shock, anger, and then some fear for your teen's future. All of that is normal and healthy.

My encouragement is to always consider your choices wisely, with counsel from godly friends. Allow the full force of your teen's consequences be her teacher; you be her supporter. And remember that God makes good on His promise to work all things together for good—in His time. He can be trusted with the outcomes of even the most shocking news, like pregnancy, alcohol and drug use, arrests, DUIs, same-sex attraction, emotional problems, and abuse. You never expect these things to happen, and when they do, you feel as if you'll never be able to crawl out of the hole they have created in your heart. But God is with you, He is with your teen, and He will see you through.

Scripture for the Day

"He will have no fear of bad news; his heart is steadfast, trusting in the Lord." (Psalm 112:7)

Thought for the Day

God promises to turn ashes into beauty, sadness into joy, and mourning into dancing. He certainly won't ignore your pain and your situation.

One Teen, Two Homes

If you have been divorced, you may struggle with sending your teen off for a weekend to the other parent's home, where the rules and beliefs may be different. Your teen may enjoy living in a rule-free environment for a while, but as he grows up, he will gravitate toward the parent he believes wants the best for him.

Maintaining consistency can be difficult, but be careful not to change the boundaries, rules, and consequences in your home just to make it a more attractive place for your child to land. Regardless of what the other parent does, keep your child's best interests at heart by providing the stability of structure and personal responsibility. Kids are resilient in these situations and will appreciate parents who are looking out for their best interests, rather than parents who are just trying to look good. Someday your teen will look back and be thankful that you helped him get to a good place.

Scripture for the Day

"Everything that was written in the past was written to teach us, so that through endurance and the encouragement of the Scriptures we might have hope. May the God who gives endurance and encouragement give you a spirit of unity among yourselves as you follow Christ Jesus." (Romans 15:4-6)

Thought for the Day

Be the person you know you should be even when it would be easier to be someone else.

Restless Parents

Sometimes I can be a little obnoxious about cleanliness. I admit it—I'm a clean freak. I'm not sure why I want everything so neat and tidy. Maybe I like to have control over at least one thing in my life.

The same may be true for you. But your restlessness can make everyone else in your family uneasy—especially your teenager. Places of refuge for your teen are few and far between. So try today to focus your energies on making your home a place of rest and unconditional acceptance for your teenager. Better to have a restful but slightly less tidy home than a picture-perfect place where no one wants to be.

Scripture for the Day

"Martha was distracted by all the preparations that had to be made. She came to [Jesus] and asked, 'Lord, don't you care that my sister has left me to do the work by myself? Tell her to help me!' 'Martha, Martha,' the Lord answered, 'you are worried and upset about many things, but only one thing is needed. Mary has chosen what is better, and it will not be taken away from her.'" (Luke 10:40-42)

Thought for the Day

I've never heard of a teen dying of a messy room. You and your teen have more important things to talk about than an unmade bed and clothes on the floor.

Struggling Teen

Teens appreciate parents who admit they're imperfect, who love unconditionally, and who say no when they need to.

I used to believe that a foolproof formula for successful parenting was based on doing certain things, like having daily family devotions, attending church together, and being involved in a youth group. Those are all important things for teens, but they aren't foolproof. I began to question the guaranteed success of the formula when I saw families who did all of these things religiously and still had a struggling teen. Today, I know that the best model for parenting is the practice of grace. Applying grace, mercy, and truth in the face of imperfections is a much better formula than the one I once believed in.

Scripture for the Day

"The God of peace will soon crush Satan under your feet. The grace of our Lord Jesus be with you." (Romans 16:20)

Thought for the Day

I've been told I'm full of a lot of things, like beans, hot air, and myself. I'd like to be full of grace.

Question for the Day

What are you full of?

Move-On Parenting

The culture is constantly changing, and so are your teen's needs. Are you adapting your style of parenting in order to meet the demands of each new season? We need to reexamine the way we communicate with our teens in order to reach them effectively. We need to move on...

from telling to sharing

from lecturing to discussing

from entertaining to experiencing things together

from demanding obedience to asking for ideas

from seeking justice to giving more grace

from giving our opinion to waiting to be invited

from punishing to allowing consequences to teach

from discouraging bad behavior to encouraging good behavior

When your teen sees you move on, she will be encouraged to move on to maturity—a priceless move that parents who aren't willing to move on may never get to see.

Scripture for the Day

"Therefore let us leave the elementary teachings about Christ and go on to maturity." (Hebrews 6:1)

Thought for the Day

We have a great message for our teens, but it won't do them any good if we aren't able to communicate it in a way they are willing to receive.

Teen
Anger

Teens who think they can get away with physically abusing you or your home need to hear a different message. If your home has become a domestic fight club, I recommend you communicate a message like this to your teen immediately: "Son, if you ever get physical with anyone in our family or destroy property in our home, you will be arrested."

That's it. No excuses, no hesitations, no trying to work around it. The message is this: "We don't get physical—period." Physical violence and verbal attacks have no place in the home. If either is going on, bring it to an abrupt halt before it develops into a lifestyle of abuse.

Scripture for the Day

"'In your anger do not sin': Do not let the sun go down while you are still angry, and do not give the devil a foothold." (Ephesians 4:26-27)

Thought for the Day

Teens who get physical usually don't have the verbal skills to communicate their feelings, so they resort to physical interaction. Not a good alternative. Stop that behavior at all costs, and start finding opportunities to help your teen express himself appropriately.

Prayer for the Day

Heavenly Father, help me stop the physical interaction and calm the outbursts with silence and humility.

Parenting Without Regrets

Physical conditioning can sometimes be painful, but it gets you in shape and prepares you to compete. The pain is a relatively small price to pay for the benefits.

Sadly, some parents won't enforce discipline because their teens may suffer some temporary emotional pain. But if you don't deal with your teen's poor thinking and bad decisions now, she will have to deal with them later, when she is no longer in your home and when the pain will undoubtedly be significantly worse.

Parenting without regrets requires disciplining a teen now in order to prepare her for the future. Today's uncomfortable consequences will most certainly become tomorrow's beneficial legacy for your teen, her children, and her grandchildren. That is something she will never regret.

Scripture for the Day

"No discipline seems pleasant at the time, but painful. Later on, however, it produces a harvest of righteousness and peace for those who have been trained by it." (Hebrews 12:11)

Prayer for the Day

Lord, help me train, correct, and teach my teen, even when doing so brings some pain. Give us strength to persevere now so that she—and her children and grandchildren—won't have to experience worse pain later.

Parental Anger

Getting angry sometimes is an important part of being human. It shows you what you really care about. Parenting can be frustrating, especially when your teenager does something stupid or when you feel that all your efforts just aren't helping your teen in life. When we get angry, we show our teenagers how to deal with anger, for better or worse. We parents need to express our anger appropriately—even our anger with God—but stuffing our anger and frustration or taking them out on our teens, spouses, or anyone else (even the dog) is not okay.

So step away and talk to God about it. Yell or scream if you need to. He is a big God, a mighty God. He can take it, and He'll show you the right way to work through your anger. Teens learn to deal with anger by imitating their parents, so lead the way in moments of anger by taking it to God instead of stuffing it or taking it out on them.

Scripture for the Day

"The LORD is compassionate and gracious, slow to anger, abounding in love." (Psalm 103:8)

Thought for the Day

Anger has an amazing way of showing you what you really want and usually arises when you have an unmet need, desire, or expectation. It's like a warning light in your car.

Question for the Day

What is your anger telling you? What do you want that you're not getting?

The Answer to Our Prayers

Do you ever ask God for a deeper relationship with Him or to become more like Him? God seems to teach by life experience, so when we ask Him for relational closeness and such traits as patience and grace, we'll undoubtedly be tested in those areas. And that's where teenagers come in. God can use your teen's antics to turn you into a better person. In fact, parenting rebellious teens can teach us more about life and God's grace than just about any other experience.

I believe that God causes some of these learning experiences, allows all of them, and uses each one to bring us the comfort, maturity, and closeness we've been seeking from Him. Christlikeness doesn't come cheap, but it's well worth the price.

Scripture for the Day

"He knows the way that I take; when he has tested me, I will come forth as gold." (Job 23:10)

Thought for the Day

Anything that comes to you has first passed through God's hands. And everything that touches you, He uses to transform you more into His image. So look for God in all situations. He hasn't forgotten you or left you.

Prayer for the Day

Lord, today, help me put a smile on my face because of Your involvement with me.

Teaching Teens to Reason

All teenagers seek more freedom as they get older. Wise parents see this as natural and healthy, and they gradually let go of the reins.

I'm not suggesting you allow your teen to go to riskier places or participate in inappropriate activities. But instead of automatically saying no, begin having thoughtful conversations with him about his requests. Most teens want their parents to help them make good decisions. So begin a dialogue. Talk through his reasoning and yours. Ask your teen good, open-ended questions and allow him to talk. Use your best listening skills. You must sign off on his final decision, but you can use such situations to help your teen think through his choices and learn how to reason.

Scripture for the Day

"Now this is what the LORD Almighty says: 'Give careful thought to your ways.'" (Haggai 1:5)

Thought for the Day

A goal of parenting isn't to give up control but to transfer control. That goal never changes, but the ways you engage with your teen must constantly adapt as his world expands and changes, his abilities develop, and he becomes responsible for his own life.

Prayer for the Day

Lord, setting my teen free is scary for me. Help me be reasonable—for his sake and mine.

Teen Loss and Anger

When teens are in emotional pain, they may attempt to deal with it by resorting to dangerous or self-destructive behavior. This may seem baffling to us at first, but think again. How can teens know how to deal with their pain in helpful ways unless we teach them? We are afraid of struggle, so we label it as bad instead of giving our teens permission to struggle constructively. They flounder through their problems because we haven't taught them how to face their pain courageously and respond to their challenges appropriately.

Teens naturally experiment, but ongoing risky behaviors related to alcohol, sex, drugs, cutting, and eating disorders often represent a teen's attempts to control or cover up painful emotions.

Nearly all teens are ill-equipped to manage emotional pain and need help dealing with it in healthy ways. If your teen is engaging in risky behavior, don't wait another minute—find a good counselor who can help her face her emotional hurts and deal with them safely. In the meantime, let her watch you as you face your own hurts honestly and grow through them.

Scripture for the Day

"We are hard pressed on every side, but not crushed; perplexed, but not in despair; persecuted, but not abandoned; struck down, but not destroyed." (2 Corinthians 4:8-9)

Question for the Day

How do you handle loss and anger? Has your child seen you work through these emotions? Is your example teaching her how to struggle well?

Teen
Self-Control

When you set up boundaries, including rules and consequences for breaking them, you maintain sanity in your home and keep it from becoming either a prison or a free-for-all. In addition, you help your teen learn the difference between right and wrong, and you give him opportunities to make choices and consider the consequences.

Boundaries give your teenager freedom to roam safely, mark the lines that he must not cross, and teach him to live a responsible, self-controlled life.

Scripture tells us that "In his heart a man plans his course, but the LORD determines his steps" (Proverbs 16:9). Similarly, you can let your teen plan his course while you guide his steps. It might look like this:

"Oh, so this is what you've decided to do. Here is how we can get there."

"So you want to go to this school. Here's how I can help with your plans."

"You want more freedom? I think you're ready. Here's how we can make it work."

"You're right—you need transportation. Let's talk about how you can get a car."

Scripture for the Day

"The fruit of the Spirit is love, joy, peace, patience, kindness, goodness, faithfulness, gentleness, and self-control." (Galatians 5:22-23)

A Parent's Fading Halo

Almost every young child thinks her parents can do no wrong. But when she reaches the teen years, her parents' halos tend to fade. You always knew you weren't perfect, but now your child is beginning to perceive reality a little more accurately as well, and she may be taking pot shots at your halo. Don't pretend your teen can't see your imperfections (she can) and don't get too upset when she points them out (she will). Just smile and agree! In fact, tell her about some of the stupid things you've done in the past. She may be shocked to hear you admit your failings, and she might become more willing to share some of her own imperfections too.

This can go a long way toward deepening your relationship with her. She'll see you as more honest, understanding, and trustworthy. She'll also learn how to process her own imperfections, which are currently dominating her thoughts thanks to her not-so tactful classmates, her acne-covered face, and her developing body.

It's a tough time to live through. Assure your teen that you lived through those difficult years too and that you're still dealing with your imperfections. Your realistic assessment of yourself and your good-natured response to your shortcomings will give her the tools she needs to maintain a healthy concept of herself.

Prayer for the Day

Lord, help me admit my faults so my teen feels free to admit hers. Help me laugh at my imperfections so she can learn to laugh at hers. And help me comfort her when others point out her flaws. May I give her an example to follow when she points out mine.

Parents Are Teachers Too

Because you are a parent, you are also a teacher. Your assignment is to teach your teen to run life's race, so be careful not to give up this teaching role too soon. Your teenager needs your wisdom more now than ever before. Just when you finish one lesson with your teen, another one springs up. The learning opportunities you share with your teen today will help him now and continue to bear fruit when he goes off to college, meets your future daughter-in-law, has kids, starts a new job, buys a house, or purchases his first car. Likewise, he'll draw on these lessons—and probably look to you for more guidance—if he ever suffers a divorce, loses a child, gets fired from a job, loses a house, has a car accident, or struggles through a difficult time.

So don't resign your teaching position too early. Your teen wants more freedom and more time with his friends, but he will also need *your* time and guidance for many years to come.

Scripture for the Day

"Fix these words of mine in your hearts and minds...Teach them to your children, talking about them when you sit at home and when you walk along the road, when you lie down and when you get up." (Deuteronomy 11:18-19)

Prayer for the Day

Lord, please give me insight into my teen's life. Show me wisdom that I can share with him. And give me the opportunities to share my heart at just the right time.

Gracious Parenting

'**ve learned that truly forgiving someone takes a lot of practice and that offering grace is not always easy. Giving something to my teen when she offends, betrays, or lies feels unnatural—and for good reason. It goes against my nature. I'm usually more interested in justice than grace.

We love to talk about God's grace—until our teens mess up royally. They may not deserve or even want forgiveness, but that may be exactly the right time to give it to them. Grace is a costly gift, and it is most needed when it is least deserved. Given appropriately and at the right moment, grace has the power to transform a relationship with a teen, just as the undeserved grace we receive from our heavenly Father transforms and renews us.

We can extend grace even as we enforce the consequences of our teens' inappropriate behavior. We do it by affirming our relationship with them at a time when they might be afraid that relationship is in jeopardy.

Scripture for the Day

"Let your conversation be always full of grace, seasoned with salt, so that you may know how to answer everyone." (Colossians 4:6)

Question for the Day

If our teens never experience grace from their earthly fathers, how will they ever recognize or learn to receive grace from their heavenly Father?

Angry Answers

Your teen probably has a unique ability to stir up your anger. He may make you mad, get you flustered, disappoint you, break the rules, be dishonest, and perhaps have bouts of disrespect. When that happens, you face a moment of truth. The way you respond will make all the difference in your relationship with him.

Police officers are trained never to lose their cool. If a traffic cop gets angry with a speeder, the offender will just get angry in return, and the officer may lose his position of authority. But when the officer calmly writes the ticket and sends the speeder on his way, the offender focuses on his stupid mistake, not on the officer.

The next time you feel anger with your teen, think of the traffic cop. Keep calm and apply the consequences, which will direct the teen's anger at his actions, not at you. Your response will help him learn, and it will also keep the lines of communication open between you and your teen.

Scripture for the Day

"Therefore, prepare your minds for action; be self-controlled; set your hope fully on the grace to be given you when Jesus Christ is revealed." (1 Peter 1:13)

Thought for the Day

We feel angry when we don't get what we want. When you get angry at your teen, consider what you're not getting, and calmly talk with your teen about what you want from him and for him.

Faithful Love

Are you ever afraid that your teen will do something that will leave a lifelong scar on her soul? A surprise pregnancy, a DUI, an ill-advised marriage, experimentation with drugs or alcohol, a season of apostasy...these could change the course of her life. But even when your teen has done the worst, she needs to know you love her just as much as you did before she made her first mistake. She needs affirmation that you will continue to be a shelter in her time of need and that your love for her will never stop, regardless of the awful consequences of her actions. When times are at their worst, you can give your child a taste of the love of God and the saving power of Jesus, who, like you, will never leave or forsake her regardless of what she's done. You can also gently lead her toward a better way of living and a different view of life.

Loving our teens can be difficult when we don't seem to receive love in return. Being respectful is tough when our teens are disrespectful. And moving toward our teens can be a challenge when they seem to be moving away. But when our love is empowered by God's Holy Spirit, it will eventually win out because of its unending source.

Scripture for the Day

"The Lord delights in those who fear him, who put their hope in his unfailing love." (Psalm 147:11)

Prayer for the Day

Jesus, help me to live and love as You did—when it's easy and when it's not.

Worry's Wrong Assumptions

Most of our worries are based on creative but faulty suppositions. Therefore, worry is usually a counterproductive misuse of our imaginations. Worry assumes things like these:

Your teen's bad behavior will never end.

God is out of touch or not in control.

You know the cause of your teen's misbehavior.

God can't be trusted or doesn't care.

When you start to worry, take a moment to write down the assumptions behind your fears. When you discover an assumption that's not true, write down something you know is true. Finally, focus on the truth, not on the assumptions, and make courageous decisions accordingly. Your teen deserves that from you.

Scripture for the Day

"Therefore I tell you, do not worry about your life, what you will eat or drink; or about your body, what you will wear... Your heavenly Father knows that you need them." (Matthew 6:25, 32)

Question for the Day

What do you worry about the most? What lies are feeding those worries? What truths can you focus on today that will help you use your imagination more productively?

Thought for the Day

All parents worry about their teens, but our heavenly Father cares for our teens more than we do.

Teen
Self-Awareness

Young children generally don't care what others think. But about the time kids start experiencing a bunch of other changes during adolescence, they quit caring about what Mom and Dad think and focus on other people's opinions. This is part of their search for identity. Carefree living is suddenly overcome by brutal self-awareness. So when your teen's behavior becomes unlike anything you've seen before, remember that he is thinking about himself in a new way. He may feel rejected by others or not know how to fit in. And when he becomes frustrated by his new self-awareness, try not to focus on his behavior. Instead, try to understand its roots—rejection, a need to fit in, or maybe a desire for attention. If your teen doesn't feel like he belongs in one group, he'll try other groups until he finds one that fits. This is hugely motivating for him.

You can come alongside your teen and help him to find his place. He's fighting for survival (acceptance), and he won't quit until he finds it. Remember your own feelings of teen insecurity and offer loving words of encouragement, affirmation, and empathy.

Scripture for the Day

"You were separate from Christ, excluded...foreigners... without hope and without God in the world. But now in Christ Jesus you who once were far away have been brought near through the blood of Christ." (Ephesians 2:12-13)

Prayer for the Day

Lord, help me empower my teen to find his place in You and in his world.

The King
Who Never Exits

I saw Elvis in concert about six months before he died. It was a fun concert with good music, but when the concert ended and the crowd called for an encore, the announcer gave us the bad news: "The king has left the building." The show was over because the king was gone. We were left a little hanging...and "all shook up."

Unlike Elvis, Christ our King, the King of kings, promises (regardless of how tough things get), "Never will I leave you, never will I forsake you." Always remember this promise and teach it to your children every day. They need to know that our King never leaves His people and is building His kingdom. The show is never over. He'll never leave us hanging...and because He's our rock, we will never be shaken.

Scripture for the Day

"Jesus answered, 'You are right in saying I am a king.'" (John 18:37)

Thought for the Day

We are to reflect the character of God in our relationship with our kids. Do they know we will never leave them, regardless of their struggles? Friends may come and go, but teens need to know that parents have staying power and will be with them and will help them build their lives.

Prayer for the Day

Father, thank You for never leaving. May my teen always feel secure with me as I do with You.

Parent Perfectionism

Seemingly perfect people tend to think that their children need to be perfect too. But the teen years are never perfect. I worked with a girl named Laura who tried to keep up the perfect teen routine but suddenly snapped and took up lying and doing whatever she pleased. As we attempted to help Laura, I noticed that her parents seemed to criticize our every effort. I discovered for myself just how difficult it was to please them, and I could see that Laura's unhappiness was rooted in feelings of frustration and imperfection. She could never please her parents, so why even try?

If you find yourself criticizing your teen's every move, lighten up. Don't drive your teen to frustration, and be sure to balance your criticisms with positive feedback when she does things right. A wise parent will know what is important and what is not, what will make a lasting effect and what will pass, and what to address now and what to deal with later. The reason for time is so that everything doesn't happen at once. So don't try to correct everything you see that could improve. Instead, take some time to love your child through her imperfections.

Scripture for the Day

"The Lord your God is with you, he is mighty to save. He will take great delight in you, he will quiet you with his love, he will rejoice over you with singing." (Zephaniah 3:17)

Prayer for the Day

Lord, thank You for rejoicing over me! Help my teen to know that I rejoice over her as well.

Mean Teen Girls

Erika was the apple of her father's eye—his princess. She was loved, cherished, and even spoiled. But her bubble burst on her first day of middle school when other girls called her names and bullied her. Her anger and hurt spilled out after school, shocking her parents. They began protecting Erika by monitoring her e-mails, text messages, and photos. They reported harassments to the school, they discussed with Erika how her world had changed and how to handle it, and they affirmed Erika with assurances of their love.

Very few parents understand the force of this world's teen culture and the impact it is having on our girls today. It is a tsunami of meanness, sexual innuendo, and continual challenges of worth and value. If parents did understand, they would probably strive to make their home a place of safety, retreat, and refreshment, not of constant correction, nagging, and ridicule. When the pressure is high at school, the pressure should be low at home. If your teen doesn't find encouragement at home, she'll find it elsewhere.

Scripture for the Day

"I could make fine speeches against you and shake my head at you. But my mouth would encourage you; comfort from my lips would bring you relief." (Job 16:4-5)

Prayer for the Day

Lord, may the words of my mouth bring comfort to my kids.

203

Moms and Dads

Most teen behavior has two main objectives: to find significance and to feel secure. Moms and dads play different roles in helping their teens reach these goals. Moms instill a sense of value in a child, and dads tend to validate it. Moms show care and concern, and dads tend to show approval. Moms comfort, and dads push to maturity. On the other hand, moms sometimes engage and protect too much as they nurse the relationship along. Dads sometimes disengage and disapprove too quickly, or they might throw up their hands and quit when they bump into problems they don't know how to fix.

When a mom or dad is absent or incapable of delivering the proper sense of value, a child will seek validation in other places—some of them inappropriate. That's why you must be available to your teen and build a relationship with him.

Scripture for the Day

"A father to the fatherless, a defender of widows, is God in his holy dwelling." (Psalm 68:5)

Prayer for the Day

Lord, help me be the parent my teen needs me to be and to fulfill the role You have given me. Sometimes I just feel lost, so would You validate me and the role I am to play? Thank You.

Letting Anger Go

Dealing with the consequences of your teen's misbehavior is sometimes no fun. When privileges are taken away from one, everyone may pay a price. If your teen wrecks her car, gets expelled from school, or causes thousands of dollars of damage, you will probably be involved in the cleanup. Her actions sometimes determine your schedule, draw on your resources, and require you to sacrifice. When that happens, you can easily get mad at her for the inconvenience she has caused your family and for her lack of consideration. Deal with your anger on your own instead of taking it out on her. Scripture teaches us to forgive, to draw from a never-ending well of grace and mercy. Go ahead and hand out the appropriate consequences—they're necessary. But be sure to express your anger appropriately. Don't break your relationship with your teen, regardless of how much time and money it costs. This is an opportunity for you to teach and for her to learn.

Scripture for the Day

"They refused to listen and failed to remember the miracles you performed among them. They became stiff-necked and in their rebellion appointed a leader in order to return to their slavery. But you are a forgiving God, gracious and compassionate; slow to anger and abounding in love." (Nehemiah 9:17)

Prayer for the Day

Father, please help me calm my emotions, quiet my spirit, and communicate my love for my teen.

Don't Redo His Work

Do you rearrange your teen's bedroom, reorganize his backpack, or rewrite his homework? Does he feel as if you check every detail, ask investigative questions nonstop, and constantly try to reorder his life? Parents can have the very best of intentions and still be overly involved in their teens' lives. As these teens get older and desire more control of their lives, they have to pry it from their parents or fight them for it. A conflict over a teen's messy room is often a fight for control, not a lesson in neatness.

When you control your teen too much, you disrespect him. If you wonder how your teen feels about your level of involvement, just ask him. "Do you mind when I change the way you do things?" You probably already know how he will answer.

Offering advice is different from taking control, so the next time you hand over a responsibility to your teen, advise him how you would do it, and then let him complete the task in his own way.

Scripture for the Day

"Encourage the young men to be self-controlled." (Titus 2:6)

Question for the Day

How much do you control your teen's life? Why do you maintain control—for fear that he can't learn on his own? (He can.) Or that God won't guide and protect your teen and you? (He will.) Can you make a new step of trust in your relationships with God and with your teen?

A Grandfather's View of Teens

A former big-city mayor once said, "What children need most are the essentials that grandparents provide in abundance: unconditional love, kindness, patience, humor, comfort, lessons in life...and most importantly, good cookies."

As a grandfather, my heart goes out to parents who are raising their teens in today's challenging culture. Grandparents can offer hope and set an example by spending time with their grandchildren, especially in the teen years. Of course, grandparents must affirm the parents' values and directives. They can also be an additional source of grace that all teens need—especially when they're down and need to hear some affirming words from older and wiser people who know them the best and love them the most. This kind of unconditional love will provide stability and the quiet wisdom only a grandparent can provide. Teens benefit from grandparents who will always be there to bless them with good conversation, words of wisdom, and good cookies.

Scripture for the Day

"Children's children are a crown to the aged, and parents are the pride of their children." (Proverbs 17:6)

Thought for the Day

A grandchild is a reward for not killing your own kids! Grandparents can love a child in a unique way, and an extended family gives a child a sense that he belongs to something important.

Teens' Options

You can tell a child is growing up when she stops asking where she came from and starts refusing to tell where she is going. Teens are on the move from dependence to independence, and we would do well to help them in this process rather than hinder them.

Teens crave independence. The best way to motivate a stubborn teen to become more responsible is to always give her options to choose from, including options that may have negative consequences. When what she wants to do is not on your list of options, she will at least have some sense of control because she is making a choice.

Have you considered that the presence of another adult under your roof may be a little weird for you? Everyone will benefit if you can go with the flow. Move away from "my way or the highway" parenting, and provide your teen with more opportunities to choose from several wise options. As she learns to make good decisions and develops internal controls, you can give her more and more freedom.

Scripture for the Day

"Choose for yourselves this day whom you will serve...But as for me and my household, we will serve the Lord." (Joshua 24:15)

Prayer for the Day

Father, I pray for creativity and wisdom as I learn to provide my teen with good options.

Restructuring Teen Responsibility

A humorous but wise newspaper columnist once wrote, "If you want children to keep their feet on the ground, put some responsibility on their shoulders." Teens want to be significant in the lives of others, and even though I'm all for parents and teens doing activities together, sometimes teens need to do something on their own so they can develop a sense of value apart from Mom and Dad.

Too much of anything—including too much idle time or time with friends—can be bad, so I recommend balancing your teen's free time with a task that is exclusively his to handle. Make it something that has meaning, such as helping an elderly neighbor, volunteering at a hospital, going on a mission trip, working a food line at a homeless shelter, teaching a Sunday school class, or helping people in need. Give him ways to interact directly with the people he is helping, instead of just asking him to stuff envelopes or pick up trash. Meaningful responsibilities can go a long way toward bringing a sense of belonging and purpose to his life and a dose of reality to his preparation for the future.

Scripture for the Day

"Each one should use whatever gift he has received to serve others, faithfully administering God's grace in its various forms." (1 Peter 4:10-11)

Thought for the Day

Teens love their parents the most when they don't have to rely on them.

Telling Teens the Truth

Parents sometimes struggle with what to say to their teens when they have to share some bad news. Talking about a terminal illness, a dying grandparent, or an automobile accident can be intimidating.

Proverbs 26:28 says, "A lying tongue hates those it hurts, and a flattering mouth works ruin." In other words, go ahead and tell the truth. You might be tempted to think you are helping a teen by not telling her the entire story, but I assure you, it will come back to bite you one day. You will either have to live with a secret, or she'll eventually find out about it—and perhaps question whether you've been honest with her in other instances.

When a father wondered what to tell his teen about his terminal illness, I advised him as I'll advise you. Don't lie. Tell a teen the truth in age-appropriate terms. Give the truth some time to sink in, and offer updates as the disease progresses. Your teen will feel empowered because you trust her with the truth, and she'll always remember your openness and honesty.

Scripture for the Day

"Dear children, let us not love with words or tongue but with actions and in truth." (1 John 3:18)

Thought for the Day

Difficult discussions provide life-changing opportunities to grow and bond.

Opportune Moments

So many parents have asked me, "What's happening to my teen?" that I decided to make that the title of one of my books. Regardless of how well you do your job as a parent, your child is likely to experience some kind of struggle during his teen years. There are no magic formulas that will guarantee your child's smooth transition to adulthood. Good parents aren't exempt from struggles, but they respond to them with sustaining faith, grace, and perseverance. Instead of seeking a quick fix, trust that God will use turbulent times to strengthen your relationship with Him and with your teen. Devote yourself to these two things: First, trust that all you've taught your teen through the years will rise to the surface at the right time. Believe it or not, you've probably done a wonderful job teaching your teen and he's probably learned more than you think. Second, trust that God will work in your teen's life. God is with you and will do things you could never do to bring about good things in your teen's life.

Scripture for the Day

"In all my prayers for all of you, I always pray with joy because of your partnership in the gospel from the first day until now, being confident of this, that he who began a good work in you [and your teen] will carry it on to completion until the day of Christ Jesus." (Philippians 1:4-6)

Prayer for the Day

Father, with each of my teen's struggles, may I surrender to You in trust and obedience.

Hard Lessons for Teens

When a parent called to say his daughter had been arrested, I encouraged him not to cancel his weeklong business trip just so he could bail her out. Instead, I suggested that he finish what he needed to and give his daughter an opportunity to do some much-needed thinking. As she processed her unwise choices and saw firsthand that society will not tolerate wrongdoing, she might have a change of heart.

If your teenager has been openly dabbling with illegal activity and gets arrested, you may not want to bail her out immediately. Yes, it's tough not to. Chances are she is safe, she's learning about consequences, and she's getting a taste of something new that she might not want in the future. A guilty teen learns invaluable lessons from spending time in a jail cell when she's done something she knows is wrong. On the other hand, if she knows her parents will rescue her every time, she may never learn, but end up in jail again and again. A short time in jail now is much better than a longer time in prison later.

Scripture for the Day

"In my distress I called to the Lord, and he answered me." (Jonah 2:2)

Prayer for the Day

Lord, if my teen ever lands in jail, please protect her. Help me lean on You for wisdom and not do what I think would immediately solve the problem. Soften my teen's heart and strengthen mine as we both learn some new lessons.

We're Not Going to Allow Disrespect

When disrespect emerges in your relationship with your teen, it's time to make sure everyone understands the rules for fighting fairly. Disagreements are a natural and important part of healthy relationships, but your teen needs to learn how to disagree and argue with respect. Here's the kind of message you can deliver:

We love you, and that will never change, but we're not going to allow you to talk that way to us anymore. We understand your need to argue your point, but there is a better way to argue. So from now on, disrespectful words or actions will only serve to get you the opposite of what you wanted—and consequences to boot.

Respect is extremely important in your relationship with your teen, so make the consequences for disrespect serious enough for him to think twice before he speaks.

Scripture for the Day

"And whatever you do, whether in word or deed, do it all in the name of the Lord Jesus, giving thanks to God the Father through him." (Colossians 3:17)

Thought for the Day

Turnabout is fair play, right? Wrong. Even when your teen shows disrespect, don't lower yourself to his level. Instead, help him rise up to yours. When you show him respect—even when his actions seem to indicate that he doesn't deserve it—you give him an example to follow, and you show him that he matters. Respect invites mutual respect.

Giving Up to Gain

Being a parent is full of paradoxes. You often have to give up something in order to receive something better. You have to let go to strengthen relational bonds. You change your child by changing yourself. So let me ask you, what are you willing to give up so change can take place? Are you willing to give up some control and allow your teen to make some decisions? Are you willing to let go of perfectionism and let her make mistakes? Will you give up your anger and calmly enforce the consequences you have set in place? Will you let go of some of your old (and possibly outdated) habits to make room for some new ones?

When you assess your own life and make adjustments, your example gives your teen permission to change as well—to give up some of her old, inappropriate ways of thinking and acting and embrace newer, healthier habits. Nothing will empower her as much as watching you go through the same process at home!

Scripture for the Day

"Now the Lord is the Spirit, and where the Spirit of the Lord is, there is freedom. And we, who with unveiled faces all reflect the Lord's glory, are being transformed into his likeness with ever-increasing glory, which comes from the Lord, who is the Spirit." (2 Corinthians 3:17-18)

Question for the Day

What are you holding on to that is keeping you from embracing something better for you and your family? What change could you make that might spark a change in your teen?

Nagging Your Teen

Nagging is just about the worst thing you can do when trying to motivate your older teen. If anything, you take away his motivation. In fact, nagging will only drive him away from the good lessons you have taught. Many times, when wise words are smothered with nagging, they do more harm than good. Instead of nagging, let your teen learn to take more responsibility by living with the consequences of not being responsible. Your child will learn more from missing his appointments, paying overdraft charges, getting fired, or waving goodbye as his friends head off to college than he will from anything you could ever say to him.

Missing a semester of school because he didn't turn in his paperwork, or losing a job because he didn't get up on time, can teach a teen that he is responsible for what goes on in his life. So stay out of it and don't nag. Such setbacks will eventually help your teen become more responsible. And responsibility will usher in the maturity that you and your teen both desire.

Scripture for the Day

"Wives, in the same way be submissive to your husbands so that, if any of them do not believe the word, they may be won over without words by the behavior of their wives." (1 Peter 3:1)

Thought for the Day

When you feel like nagging, try being silent and letting the consequences do their work. If you step aside, your message can impact your teen and strengthen your relationship.

Not by Accident

Your teenager won't become responsible or learn to think more maturely by accident. She will learn because she has to. She learns from being in situations where responsibility and maturity are expected and modeled. That's why I highly encourage you to get your teen into a part-time job, particularly a job that is service oriented. Next to her relationship with you, nothing can teach her more about life and making a livelihood than a job can, regardless of whether she needs the money.

The right job for just a few hours each week can be a perfect place for your teen to learn about people skills, money management, and time management. It can even help her determine what she does or doesn't want to do after high school. The prodigal son came to his senses when no one was giving anything to him (Luke 15:15-17). So quit giving your teen everything and start requiring some things from her. You'll both be happier in the long run.

Scripture for the Day

"The sluggard's craving will be the death of him, because his hands refuse to work." (Proverbs 21:25)

Prayer for the Day

Lord, help me quit giving everything to my teen so that she may learn the skills she needs to succeed in life. Teach me—as I teach her—that our goal in this world is not to have everything, but to give in such a way that helps others find and know You.

Teen Selfishness

Some parents prolong their children's selfishness by continuing to do everything for them when they become teens. These parents' worlds revolve around their children, giving the kids a false sense that they are still the center of the universe as they were in their younger years.

When your teen turns fifteen, aggressively begin helping him get over a selfish mind-set. Instead of being served by Mom and Dad, he needs to begin doing things for himself and also start doing some things for others. You want your teen to learn that lesson now, instead of waiting until he gets married, right? Jesus told His disciples, "Now that I, your Lord and Teacher, have washed your feet, you also should wash one another's feet. I have set you an example that you should do as I have done for you" (John 13:14-15). Your teen is ready to learn this lesson. So put on the brakes! Stop doing everything for him, like doing his laundry, waking him up, finishing his chores, or paying for his every need. Find ways to stop taking responsibility for him so that he can start taking responsibility for himself.

Scripture for the Day

"Whoever wants to become great among you must be your servant, and whoever wants to be first must be slave of all. For even the Son of Man did not come to be served, but to serve, and to give his life as a ransom for many." (Mark 10:43-45)

Prayer for the Day

Lord, help me learn to say no to my teen. Show me ways that I can set him free to grow.

Embracing the Sinful Child

What's the best way you can help your wayward child find her way home? It's not by turning your back on her. Regardless of whether she's a teen or an adult, your love—within boundaries and without enabling sinful behavior—is the key to your influence in her life. You are not her judge and jury, so even though you don't like or approve of her sinful state, continue to love her.

Our hope is found in Philippians 1:6: "He who began a good work in you will carry it on to completion." God is not finished with your child, and He will often do His work through you. So the challenge is to not let your own attitudes, hurts, and disappointments get in the way. When your child's imperfections rise to the surface, you can let her know that you will love her when she has it together and when she doesn't. That's the way God loves you.

Scripture for the Day

"Do not be anxious about anything, but in everything, by prayer and petition, with thanksgiving, present your requests to God. And the peace of God, which transcends all understanding, will guard your hearts and your minds in Christ Jesus." (Philippians 4:6-7)

Prayer for the Day

Thank You for my teen, for You are teaching me much through her. Amen!

Don't be afraid, I've redeemed you.

I've called your name. You're mine.

When you're in over your head, I'll be there with you.

When you're in rough waters, you will not go down.

When you're between a rock and a hard place,

it won't be a dead end—

Because I am GOD, your personal God,

The Holy of Israel, your Savior.

I paid a huge price for you:

all of Egypt, with rich Cush and Seba thrown in!

That's how much you mean to me!

That's how much I love you!

I'd sell off the whole world to get you back,

trade the creation just for you.

So don't be afraid: I'm with you.

I'll round up all your scattered children,

pull them in from east and west.

I'll send orders north and south:

"Send them back.

Return my sons from distant lands,

my daughters from faraway places.

I want them back, every last one who bears my name,

every man, woman, and child

Whom I created for my glory,

yes, personally formed and made each one."

ISAIAH 43:1-7 MSG

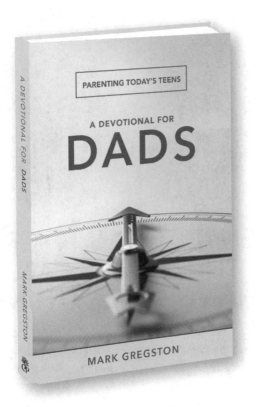

To order more copies of

A DEVOTIONAL FOR

DADS

Order online at:

- www.HeartlightMinistries.org/resources
  - or call 1-866-700-FAMILY (3264)

Also available on Amazon.com and
ChristianBook.com

WHEN IT COMES TO CRISIS,
THREE DAYS CAN
CHANGE EVERYTHING.

Are you in the middle of a family crisis? Know a family that is?
Our Families in Crisis Conference offers hope for a better future.
This three-day conference is taught and hosted by Mark Gregston,
Founder and Executive Director of Heartlight Ministries and host of
Parenting Today's Teens. Parents who attend will leave with a more
complete understanding of how to influence real change and help
lost teens find their way back on track.

The event is held on the beautiful Heartlight campus,
about 150 miles east of Dallas, Texas. **To learn more and register
visit FamiliesInCrisisConference.com or call 903.668.2173.**

FAMILIES IN CRISIS
C O N F E R E N C E

Make a deeper **connection** with your teen.

For daily insights, advice and guidance find us on Facebook.

Visit Facebook.com/ParentingTeens